Important Instruction

Use the URL or QR code provided below to unlock all the online learning resources included with this Grade 5 to 6 summer learning activities workbook.

URL	QR Code
Visit the URL below for online registration **http://www.lumoslearning.com/a/tg5-6**	

Your online access includes;

- Skills practice resources for Grade 6 Math and ELA
- Grade-appropriate passages to improve reading skills
- Grade 5 vocabulary quizzes
- Access to Lumos Flashcube - An interactive tool to improve vocabulary
- Educational videos, worksheets, standards information and more

Additional Benefits of Online Registration

- Entry to Lumos Weekly Summer Photo Contest
- Entry to Lumos Short Story Competition

Lumos Learning
Developed by Expert Teachers

Summer Learning HeadStart, Grade 5 to 6: Fun Activities Plus Math, Reading, and Language Workbooks

Contributing Author   - Julie Turner
Contributing Author   - April LoTiempo
Contributing Author   - Julie C. Lyons
Contributing Editor   - George Smith
Contributing Editor   - Marisa Adams
Executive Producer   - Mukunda Krishnaswamy
Designer and Illustrator - Harini N.

First Edition - 2020

ISBN 10: 1940484715

ISBN 13: 978-1-940484-71-6

Printed in the United States of America

Last updated - April 2022

For permissions and additional information contact us

Lumos Information Services, LLC
PO Box 1575, Piscataway, NJ 08855-1575
http://www.LumosLearning.com

Email: support@lumoslearning.com
Tel: (732) 384-0146
Fax: (866) 283-6471

Developed by Expert Teachers

Table of Contents

Introduction

What is Summer Academic Learning Loss?

What is Summer Academic Learning Loss? Studies show that if students take a standardized test at the end of the school year, and then repeat that test when they return in the fall, they will lose approximately four to six weeks of learning. In other words, they could potentially miss more questions in the fall than they would in the spring. This loss is commonly referred to as the summer slide.

When these standardized testing scores drop an average of one month, it causes teachers to spend at least the first four to five weeks, on average, re-teaching critical material. In terms of math, students typically lose an average of two and a half months of skills, and when reading and math losses are combined, it averages three months; it may even be lower for students in lower-income homes.

And on average, the three areas students will typically lose ground in are spelling, vocabulary, and mathematics.

How can You Help Combat Summer Learning Loss?

Like anything, academics are something that requires practice, and if they are not used regularly, you run the risk of losing them. Because of this, it is imperative your children work to keep their minds sharp over the summer. There are many ways to keep your children engaged over the summer, and we're going to explore some of the most beneficial.

Start with School:

Your best source of information is your child's school. Have a conversation with your child's teacher. Tell them you are interested in working on some academics over the summer and ask what suggestions they might have. Be sure to ask about any areas your child may be struggling in and for a list of books to read over the summer. Also, talk to your child's counselor. They may have recommendations of local summer activities that will relate back to the schools and what your child needs to know. Finally, ask the front office staff for any information on currently existing after school programs (the counselor may also be able to provide this). Although after school programs may end shortly, the organizations running them will often have information on summer camps. Many of these are often free or at a very low cost to you and your family.

Stay Local:

Scour your local area for free or low-cost activities and events. Most museums will have dollar days of some kind where you can get money-off admission for going on a certain day of the week or a certain time. Zoos will often do the same thing. Take lunch to the park and eat outside, talking about the leaves, flowers, or anything else you can find there. Your child can pick one favorite thing and research it. Attend concerts or shows put on by local artists, musicians, or other vendors. There are many other options available; you just have to explore and find them. The key here is to engage your children. Have them look online with you or search the local newspapers/magazines. Allow them to plan the itinerary, or work with you on it, and when they get back, have them write a journal about the activity. Or, even better, have them write a letter or email to a family member about what they did.

Practice Daily:

Whether the choice is a family activity or experiencing the local environment, staying academically focused is the key is to keep your child engaged every day. This daily practice helps keep student's minds sharp and focused, ensuring they will be able to not only retain the knowledge they have learned, but in many cases begin to move ahead for the next year.

Summer Strategies for Students

Summer is here, which brings a time of excitement, relaxation, and fun. School is the last thing on your mind, but that doesn't mean learning has to be on vacation too. In fact, learning is as just as important and be just as fun (if not more) during the summer months than during the school year.

Did you know that during the summer:

- Students often lose an average of 2 and ½ months of math skills
- Students often lose 2 months of reading skills
- Teachers spend at least the first 4 to 5 weeks of the next school year reteaching important skills and concepts

Your brain is like a muscle, and like any muscle, it must be worked out regularly, and like this, your language arts and math skills are something that requires practice; if you do not use them regularly, you run the risk of losing them. So, it is very important you keep working through the summer. But, it doesn't always have to be 'school' type of work. There are many ways to stay engaged, and we're going to spend a little time looking through them.

Read and Write as Often as Possible

Reading is one of the most important things you can do to keep your brain sharp and engaged. Here are some tips to remember about summer reading:

- Often, summer is the perfect time to find and read new books or books you have always been curious about. However, without your teacher, you may struggle with finding a book that is appropriate for your reading level. In this case, you just have to remember the five-finger rule: open a book to a random page and begin reading aloud, holding up one finger for each word you cannot say or do not know. If you have more than five fingers visible, then the book is probably too hard to read.

- Reading goes beyond books; there are so many other ways to read. Magazines are a great way to keep kids connected to learning, and they encourage so many different activities. National Geographic Kids, Ranger Rick, and American Girl are just a few examples. As silly as it may sound, you can also read the backs of cereal boxes and billboards to work on reading confidence and fluency, and learn many new things along the way! And thinking completely outside the box, you can also read when singing karaoke. Reading the words as they flash across the screen is a great way to build fluency. You can also turn the closed captioning on when a TV show is on to encourage literacy and reading fluency.

But writing is equally as important, and there are many things you can do to write over the summer:

- First, consider keeping a journal of your summer activities. You can detail the things you do, places you go, even people you meet. Be sure to include as much description as possible – sights, sounds, colors should all be included so you can easily remember and visualize the images. But the wonderful thing about a journal is that spelling and sentence structure are not as important. It's just the practice of actually writing;   that is where your focus should be. The other nice thing about a journal is that this informal writing is just for you; with journal writing you don't have to worry about anything, you just have to start writing.

- But if you want a little more depth to your journaling, and you want to share it with others, there is a fantastic opportunity for you with blogging. With parental approval, you can create a blog online where you can share your summer experiences with friends, family, or any others. The wonderful thing about blogs is that you can play with the privacy settings and choose whom you want to see your blogs. You can make it private, where only the individuals who you send the link to can see it, or you can choose for it to be public where anyone can read it. Of course, if you are keeping a blog, you will have to make it a little more formal and pay attention to spelling, grammar, and sentences simply because you want to make sure your blog is pleasing to those who are reading it. Some popular places to post blogs are Blogger, Wordpress, Squarespace, and Quillpad.

Practice Math in Real Life

One way you can keep your brain sharp is by looking at the world around you and finding ways to include math. In this case, we're thinking of fun, practical ways to practice in your daily life.

- First, have some fun this summer with being in charge of some family projects. Suggest a fun project to complete with a parent or grandparent; decide on an area to plant some new bushes or maybe a small home project you can work on together. You can help design the project and maybe even research the best plants to plant or the best way to build the project. Then write the shopping list, making sure you determine the correct amount of supplies you will need. Without even realizing it, you would have used some basic math calculations and geometry to complete the project.

- You can also find math in shopping for groceries or while doing some back to school shopping. For each item that goes into the cart, estimate how much it will be and keep a running estimation of the total cost. Make it a competition before you go by estimating what your total bill will be and see who comes the closest. Or, you can even try and compete to see who can determine the correct total amount of tax that will be needed. And a final mental game to play while shopping is to determine the change you should receive when paying with cash. Not only is this a good skill to practice math, more importantly, helps you make sure you're getting the correct change.

- You can even use everyday math if you are doing any traveling this summer, and there are many fun ways to do this. Traveling requires money, and someone has to be in charge of the budget. You can volunteer to be the family accountant. Make a budget for the trip and keep all the receipts. Tally up the cost of the trip and even try to break it up by category – food, fun, hotels, gas are just a few of the categories you can include. For those of you who might be looking for even more of a challenge, you can calculate what percentage of your budget has been spent on each category as well.

- And traveling by car gives many opportunities as well. Use the car odometer to calculate how far you have traveled. For an added challenge, you can see if you can calculate how much gas you used as well as how many gallons of gas per mile have been used.

Practice Daily:

Whether the choice is a family activity or experiencing the local environment, staying academically focused is the key to keep your mind engaged every day. That daily practice keeps your brain sharp and focused, and helps to ensure that you are not only able to retain the knowledge you learned last year but also to get a jump start on next year's success too!

This book offers a variety of state standards aligned resources, in both printed and online format, to help students learn during Summer months.

The activities in the book are organized by week and aligned with the 5th-grade learning standards. We encourage you to start at the beginning of Summer holidays. During each week, students can complete daily Math and English practice. There are five daily practice worksheets for each week. Students can log in to the online program once a week to complete reading, vocabulary and writing practice. Students can work on fun activity anytime during that week. Additionally, students can record their Summer activity through the online program.

Please note that the online program also includes access to 6th grade learning resources. This section of the online program could be used to help students to get a glimpse of what they would be learning in the next grade level.

Weekly Fun Summer Photo Contest

Take a picture of your summer fun activity and share it on Twitter or Instagram

Use the **#SummerLearning** mention

@LumosLearning on Twitter or

@lumos.learning on Instagram

Tag friends and increase your chances of winning the contest

Participate and stand a chance to WIN $50 Amazon gift card!

Take Advantage of the Online Resources

To access the online resources included with this book, parents and teachers can register with a FREE account. With each free signup, student accounts can be associated to enable online access for them.

Once the registration is complete, the login credentials for the created accounts will be sent in email to the id used during signup. Students can log in to their student accounts to get started with their summer learning. Parents can use the parent portal to keep track of student's progress.

URL	QR Code
Visit the URL below for online registration **http://www.lumoslearning.com/a/tg5-6**	

Lumos Short Story Competition 2022

Write a Short Story
Based On Your Summer Experiences

Get A Chance To Win $100 Cash Prize
+
1 Year Free Subscription To Lumos StepUp
+
Trophy With Certificate

How can my child participate in this competition?

Step 1
Visit **www.lumoslearning.com/a/tg5-6** to register for online fun summer program.

Step 2
After registration, your child can upload their summer story by logging into the student portal and clicking on Lumos Short Story Competition 2022.
Last date for submission is August 31, 2022

How is this competition judged?
Lumos teachers will review students submissions in Sep 2022. Quality of submission would be judged based on creativity, coherence and writing skills.

We recommend short stories that are less than 500 words.

Week 1 Summer Practice

Write and Interpret Numerical Expressions (5.OA.A.1)

1. Evaluate the expression (8 x 6) + (8-3)?

    $48 + 5$

    ● 53
    Ⓑ 48
    Ⓒ 64
    Ⓓ 81

2. Where must the parenthesis be in the following expression so that the answer is 6?
    20 - 8 ÷ 2

    Ⓐ 20 - (8 ÷ 2)
    Ⓑ (20 - 8) ÷ 2

3. Evaluate the expression 4 x (2 + 1) + 6

    Ⓐ 18
    Ⓑ 15
    Ⓒ 21
    Ⓓ 16

4. What is the value of 2 x [5-(6 ÷3)]?

    $2 \times [5 - 2]$

    6

Day 1

What is this life if, full of care,
We have no time to stand and stare?

No time to stand beneath the boughs
And stare as long as sheep or cows.

No time to see, when woods we pass,
Where squirrels hide their nuts in grass

No time to see, in broad daylight,
Streams full of stars, like skies at night.

No time to turn at Beauty's glance,
And watch her feet, how they can dance.

No time to wait till her mouth can
Enrich that smile her eyes began.

A poor life if, full of care,
We have no time to stand and stare.

-- W. H. Davies

5. Where can you find the answer to the question in the first stanza?

Ⓐ In the first stanza
Ⓑ In the fourth stanza
Ⓒ In the last stanza
Ⓓ The poet does not answer the question.

Once there was a severe drought. There was little water in Tony's well, and he didn't know what would happen to the fruit trees in his garden. Just then, he noticed three men looking intently at his house. He was certain that the three strangers were planning to rob his house. He acted quickly. He shouted out to his son, "My son, due to the drought, money has become scarce. There are many thieves. Let us protect our valuables, and put all of our jewels in a box and throw them into the well. They will be safe there." He quickly told his son to put some large stones in a box and throw them into the well. The thieves heard the sound of the box falling into the well and were happy.

That night they came to the well. The box was heavy and had landed deep down in the well. To get it, they would have to take out some of the water. They started drawing water from the well and pouring it onto the ground. Tony had made arrangements to make sure that the water reached his fruit trees. He had channels leading from the well to each of the trees.

By the time thieves found the box, they had drawn out enough water to water the trees. It was almost dawn. Tony sent for the soldiers, and just as the thieves were trying to open the box, they were caught red-handed.

6. What would be an appropriate title for the above story?

Ⓐ "Cunning Tony"
Ⓑ "The Thieves"
Ⓒ "The Well"
Ⓓ "A Clever Idea"

7. What did Tony secretly ask his son to do?

Ⓐ To put the clothes in the box
Ⓑ To put the jewels in the box
Ⓒ To put the papers in the box
Ⓓ To put large stones in the box

8. Part A

What is the main purpose of the first paragraph in the above story?
Ⓐ It introduces us to the story and the characters in the story.
Ⓑ It introduces us to the situation in the story.
Ⓒ It lays the setting or the foundation for the story.
Ⓓ All of the above.

8. Part B

Which details in the above story tells us that the country was going through a difficult time?

Ⓐ Once there was a severe drought.
Ⓑ There was little water in Tony's well.
Ⓒ He shouted out to his son, "My son, because of the drought, money has become scarce."
Ⓓ All of the above.

Challenge Yourself!

- **Write and Interpret Numerical Expressions**
- **Supporting Statements**

https://www.lumoslearning.com/a/dc5-1

Day 1

See Page 7 for Signup details

Day 2

1. Which expression shows 10 more than the "quotient" of 72 "divided" by 8?

    Ⓐ (10 + 72) ÷ 8
    Ⓑ (72 ÷ 8) + 10
    Ⓒ 72 ÷ (8 + 10)
    Ⓓ 8 ÷ (72 + 10)

2. Which expression shows 75 minus the product of 12 and 4?

    Ⓐ (75 – 12) x 4
    Ⓑ (12 x 4) – 75
    Ⓒ 75 – (12 + 4)
    Ⓓ 75 – (12 x 4)

3. Jamie purchased 10 cases of soda for a party. Each case holds 24 cans. He also purchased 3 packs of juice. Each pack of juice has 6 cans. Which expression represents the number of cans he purchased?

    Ⓐ (10 x 24) + (3 x 6)
    Ⓑ (10 + 24) x (3 + 6)
    Ⓒ 10 x (24 + 6)
    Ⓓ 10 x 24 x 3 x 6

4. **Part A**
    Which of these expressions would result in the greatest number?

    Ⓐ 420 – (28 x 13)
    Ⓑ 420 + 28 + 13
    Ⓒ (420 – 28) x 13
    Ⓓ 420 + (28 x 13)

    Part B
    Which of these expressions would result in the smallest number?

    Ⓐ 684 – (47 + 6)
    Ⓑ 684 – 47 – 6
    Ⓒ (684 – 47) x 6
    Ⓓ 684 – (47 x 6)

A Clever Idea

Once there was a severe drought. There was little water in Tony's well, and he didn't know what would happen to the fruit trees in his garden. Just then, he noticed three men looking intently at his house. He was certain that the three strangers were planning to rob his house. He acted quickly. He shouted out to his son, "My son, due to the drought, money has become scarce. There are many thieves. Let us protect our valuables, and put all of our jewels in a box and throw them into the well. They will be safe there." He quickly told his son to put some large stones in a box and throw them into the well. The thieves heard the sound of the box falling into the well and were happy.

That night they came to the well. The box was heavy and had landed deep down in the well. To get it, they would have to take out some of the water. They started drawing water from the well and pouring it onto the ground. Tony had made arrangements to make sure that the water reached his fruit trees. He had channels leading from the well to each of the trees.

By the time thieves found the box, they had drawn out enough water to water the trees. It was almost dawn. Tony sent for the soldiers, and just as the thieves were trying to open the box, they were caught red-handed.

5. The above passage is about _____.

Ⓐ how the thieves watered the field.
Ⓑ how the thieves robbed for money.
Ⓒ how the thieves took the jewels.
Ⓓ how the thieves put the box in the well.

6. Part A
Why did Tony throw a box of stones down the well?

Ⓐ The stones were valuable to Tony.
Ⓑ The stones were worth a fortune.
Ⓒ The stones were a diversion.
Ⓓ There was no money at all.

Part B
Why did Tony send for soldiers?

Ⓐ Tony worked for the Army.
Ⓑ They enforced the laws of the area.
Ⓒ The police were stealing the jewels.
Ⓓ Tony trusted the thieves.

Do Your Best

Katie stood before the crowd blushing and wringing her hands. She looked out and saw the room full of faces. Some she knew and some she did not, but they were all here to listen to her. Taking a deep breath, she opened her mouth, but no words came out. Tears formed in the corners of her eyes as she closed them.

With her eyes closed, she imagined her mother helping her get dressed and ready for tonight. "Just do your best," is what her mother had told her.

She opened her eyes and found her mother's smiling face in the crowd. Relaxing, she took another deep breath and started singing. She did not stop until she finished, and the crowd was on their feet applauding.

After the show, she found her parents and her friends. They all had wonderful things to say about her song and how proud they were because she kept going even when it seemed like she might give up. She shrugged her shoulders and shared a smile with her mother.

"I just did my best," she answered.

7. The above passage is about _____.

- Ⓐ being determined
- Ⓑ giving up
- Ⓒ listening to friends
- Ⓓ taking a deep breath

8. At the beginning of the story, how was Katie feeling?

- Ⓐ Katie was friendly.
- Ⓑ Katie was excited.
- Ⓒ Katie was depressed.
- Ⓓ Katie was nervous.

Challenge Yourself!

- **Record & Interpret Calculations with Numbers**
- **Drawing Inferences**

https://www.lumoslearning.com/a/dc5-2

Day 2

See Page 7 for Signup details

1. **Which set of numbers completes the function table?**
    Rule: multiply by 3

Input	Output
1	☐
2	☐
5	15
8	☐
12	☐

Ⓐ 4, 5, 11, 15
Ⓑ 3, 6, 24, 36
Ⓒ 3, 6, 32, 48
Ⓓ 11, 12, 18, 112

2. **Which set of numbers completes the function table?**
    Rule: add 4, then divide by 2

Input	Output
4	☐
6	☐
10	7
22	☐
40	☐

Ⓐ 1, 3, 19, 37
Ⓑ 10, 12, 28, 46
Ⓒ 4, 5, 13, 22
Ⓓ 16, 20, 52, 88

3.   Which set of coordinate pairs matches the function table?
        Rule: multiply by 2, then subtract 1

Input	Output
5	☐
9	17
14	☐
25	☐

Ⓐ (5 , 9), (9 , 17), (14 , 27), (25 , 49)
Ⓑ (5 , 9), (14 , 25), (9 , 17), (27 , 49)
Ⓒ (5 , 9), (9 , 17), (17 , 14), (14 , 25)
Ⓓ (5 , 11), (9 , 17), (14 , 29), (25 , 51)

4.   Consider the following pattern:
     7, 9, 4, 6, 1, . . .

     If the pattern continued, what would be the first negative number to appear?

     Write your answer in the box given below.

Katie stood before the crowd blushing and wringing her hands. She looked out and saw the room full of faces. Some she knew and some she did not, but they were all here to listen to her. Taking a deep breath, she opened her mouth, but no words came out. Tears formed in the corners of her eyes as she closed them.

With her eyes closed, she imagined her mother helping her get dressed and ready for tonight. "Just do your best," is what her mother had told her. She opened her eyes and found her mother's smiling face in the crowd. Relaxing, she took another deep breath and started singing. She did not stop until she finished, and the crowd was on their feet applauding.

After the show, she found her parents and her friends. They all had wonderful things to say about her song and how proud they were because she kept going even when it seemed like she might give up. She shrugged her shoulders and shared a smile with her mother. "I just did my best," she answered.

5. Choose a suitable title for this story.

Ⓐ "Trust People"
Ⓑ "Listening to Mom"
Ⓒ "Do Your Best"
Ⓓ "The Show"

6. What is the overall theme of this story?

Ⓐ Give up under pressure.
Ⓑ Always do your best.
Ⓒ Never let your friends get you down.
Ⓓ Close your eyes when you are getting ready to sing.

7. What can we learn from this story?

The Glass Cupboard

There was a king who had a cupboard that was made entirely of glass. It was a special cupboard. It looked empty, but you could always take out anything you wanted. There was only one thing that had to be remembered. Whenever something was taken out of it, something else had to be put back in, although nobody knew why.

One day some thieves broke into the palace and stole the cupboard. "Now, we can have anything we want," they said. One of the thieves said, "I want a large bag of gold," and he opened the glass cupboard and got it. The other two did the same, and they, too, got exactly what they wanted. The thieves forgot one thing. Not one of them put anything back inside the cupboard.

This went on and on for weeks and months. At last, the leader of the thieves could bear it no longer. He took a hammer and smashed the glass cupboard into a million pieces, and then all three thieves fell down dead.

When the king returned home, he ordered his servants to search for the cupboard. When the servants found it and the dead thieves, they filled sixty great carts with the gold and took it back to the king. He said, "If those thieves had only put something back into the cupboard, they would be alive to this day."

He ordered his servants to collect all of the pieces of glass and then melt into a globe of the world with all the countries on it. This was to remind himself and others, to give back something in return when someone shows an act of kindness or gives us something.

8. What is the purpose of this story?

Ⓐ This story is about learning how to break a glass cupboard.
Ⓑ This story is about learning the importance of gold.
Ⓒ This story is about giving something back in return.
Ⓓ This story is about a king.

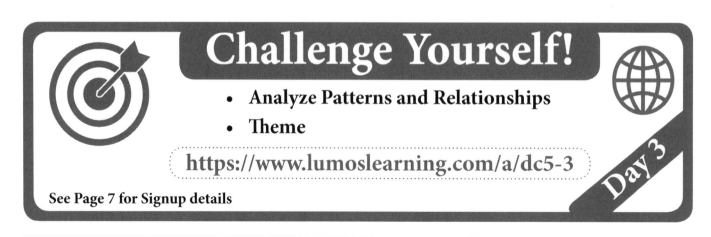

Challenge Yourself!

- **Analyze Patterns and Relationships**
- **Theme**

https://www.lumoslearning.com/a/dc5-3

See Page 7 for Signup details

Day 3

Day 4

1. In the number 913,874 which digit is in the ten thousands place?

    Ⓐ 8
    Ⓑ 1
    Ⓒ 9
    Ⓓ 3

2. In the number 7.2065 which digit is in the thousandths place?

    Ⓐ 5
    Ⓑ 2
    Ⓒ 0
    Ⓓ 6

3. Which number is equivalent to $\frac{8}{10}$?

    Ⓐ 0.8
    Ⓑ 8.0
    Ⓒ 0.08
    Ⓓ 0.008

4. Read each statement and indicate whether it is true or false.

	Yes	No
The 5 in 570.22 is ten times greater than 5 in 456.1.	○	○
The 8 in 2.083 is hundred times less than the 8 in 328.7.	○	○
The 3 in 1.039 is hundred times less than the 3 in 67.3.	○	○
The 2 in 9,523 is thousand times more than the 2 in 45.92	○	○

Do Your Best

Katie stood before the crowd blushing and wringing her hands. She looked out and saw the room full of faces. Some she knew and some she did not. But, they were all here to listen to her. Taking a deep breath, she opened her mouth, but no words came out. Tears formed in the corners of her eyes as she closed them.

With her eyes closed, she imagined her mother helping her get dressed and ready for tonight. "Just do your best," is what her mother had told her. She opened her eyes and found her mother's smiling face in the crowd. Relaxing, she took another deep breath and started singing. She did not stop until she finished, and the crowd was on their feet applauding.

After the show, she found her parents and her friends. They all had wonderful things to say about her song and how proud they were because she kept going even when it seemed like she might give up. She shrugged her shoulders and shared a smile with her mother. "I just did my best," she answered.

5. Who are the main characters in the above story?

- Ⓐ Katie, her mother, and her friends
- Ⓑ Katie and her mother
- Ⓒ Katie and her parents
- Ⓓ Katie and her friends

6. Who are the secondary characters is this story?

- Ⓐ Katie and her mother
- Ⓑ Katie's father and her mother
- Ⓒ Katie's father and her friends
- Ⓓ Katie and her friends

7. Part A
What does this story reveal about Katie's character?

- Ⓐ That she was a girl who gave up easily.
- Ⓑ That she was a girl who put forth effort to overcome her fears.
- Ⓒ That she had no talent at all.
- Ⓓ That she was meek and ran away from a difficult situation.

7. Part B
What does this story say about Katie's mother?

- Ⓐ She was very supportive.
- Ⓑ She was not supportive.
- Ⓒ She did not believe in singing.
- Ⓓ She wanted her daughter to make friends.

Late for School

Marrah heard the brakes on the bus as she shoveled the rest of her breakfast into her mouth. "You just missed the bus!" Marrah's mother yelled. "Why can't you ever be on time?"

"I'm sorry, Mom," Marrah sighed. She ran upstairs to her room so she could get her backpack, knowing she needed to hurry because her mother would have to take her to school.

"Let's go, Marrah!" Her mother called from downstairs. "You don't want to be late for school too!"

Frantic now, Marrah lifted her sheets to look under them before dropping to her knees in front of her bed. She pushed mounds of clothes out of the way as she continued to search for her backpack.

"Marrah!" Her mother called again, and she could hear the impatience in her mother's voice downstairs. She ran out of her room and leaned over the rail.

"I can't find my backpack!" She cried out.
"You mean this one?" Her mother pulled the bag from the floor beside her.
"Oh," she replied, her shoulders sagging as she walked down the stairs.

"Let's go to school, Marrah." Her mother said with a small smile on her face as they walked out the door.

8. In the above story, Marrah appears to be _____ .

- Ⓐ a very disorganized girl
- Ⓑ a very organized girl
- Ⓒ a very punctual girl
- Ⓓ a very disciplined girl

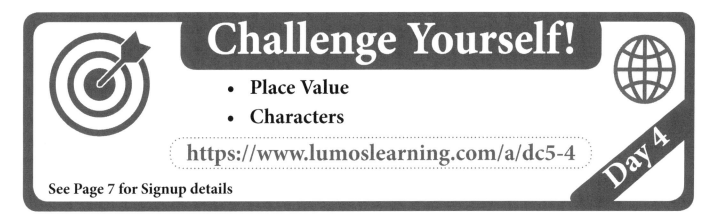

Challenge Yourself!

- **Place Value**
- **Characters**

https://www.lumoslearning.com/a/dc5-4

Day 4

See Page 7 for Signup details

Day 5

1. $9 \times 10^3 =$

    Ⓐ 900
    Ⓑ 9,000
    Ⓒ 117
    Ⓓ 270

2. What is the quotient of 10^7 divided by 100?

    Ⓐ 0.7
    Ⓑ 100,000
    Ⓒ 70,000
    Ⓓ 700

3. Solve: $0.51 \times$ ____ $= 5,100$

    Ⓐ 10^4
    Ⓑ 10^2
    Ⓒ 100
    Ⓓ 10^3

4. Write the number 1,000 as a power of ten. Enter your answer in the box given below

The Traveler

A weary traveler stopped at Sam's house and asked him for shelter for the night. Sam was a friendly soul. He not only agreed to let the traveler stay for the night; he decided to treat his guest to some curried chicken. So he bought a couple of chickens from the market and gave them to his wife to cook. Then he went off to buy some fruit.

Now, Sam's wife could not resist food. She had a habit of eating as she cooked. So as she cooked the meat, she smelled the rich steam and could not help tasting a piece. It was tender and delicious, and she decided to have another piece. Soon, there was only a tiny bit left. Her little son, Kevin, ran into the kitchen. She gave him that little piece.

Kevin found it so tasty that he begged his mother for more. But there was no more chicken left. The traveler, who had gone to have a wash, returned. The woman heard him coming and had to think of a plan quickly. She began to scold her son loudly: "Your father has taught you a shameful and disgusting habit. Stop it, I tell you!" The traveler was curious. "What habit has his father taught the child?" he asked. "Oh," said the woman, "Whenever a guest arrives, my husband cuts off their ears and roasts them for my son to eat."

The traveler was shocked. He picked up his shoes and fled.

"Why has our guest left in such a hurry?" asked Sam when he came back.

"A fine guest indeed!" exclaimed his wife. "He snatched the chickens out of my pot and ran off with them!"

"The chickens!" exclaimed Sam. He ran after his guest, shouting. "Let me have one, at least; you may keep the other!" But his guest only ran faster!

5. The above passage is about _____.

   Ⓐ   The wife who could not resist food and ate the chickens
   Ⓑ   The greedy traveler who ate all the chickens
   Ⓒ   Sam, who was a friendly soul
   Ⓓ   The son who ate the guest

THE LITTLE PINK ROSE
Best Stories to Tell to Children (1912)
By Sara Cone Bryant

Once there was a little pink Rosebud, and she lived down in a little dark house under the ground. One day she was sitting there, all by herself, and it was very still. Suddenly, she heard a little tap, tap, tap, at the door. "Who is that?" she said.

"It's the Rain, and I want to come in," said a soft, sad, little voice.

"No, you can't come in," the little Rosebud said. By and by she heard another little tap, tap, tap, on the windowpane. "Who is there?" she said.

The same soft little voice answered, "It's the Rain, and I want to come in!"

"No, you can't come in," said the little Rosebud. Then it was very still for a long time. At last, there came a little rustling, whispering sound, all around the window: rustle, whisper, whisper. "Who is there?" said the little Rosebud.

"It's the Sunshine," said a little, soft, cheery voice, "and I want to come in!"

"N -- no," said the little pink rose, "you can't come in." And she sat still again.

Pretty soon, she heard the sweet little rustling noise at the key-hole. "Who is there?" she said.

"It's the Sunshine," said the cheery little voice, "and I want to come in. I want to come in!"

No, no," said the little pink rose, "you cannot come in."

By and by, as she sat so still, she heard tap, tap, tap, and rustle, whisper, rustle, all up and down the windowpane, and on the door, and at the key-hole. "Who is there?" she said.

"It's the Rain and the Sun, the Rain and the Sun," said two little voices, together, "and we want to come in! We want to come in! We want to come in!"

"Dear, dear," said the little Rosebud, "if there are two of you, I s'pose I shall have to let you in." So she opened the door a little wee crack, and they came in. And one took one of her little hands, and the other took her other little hand, and they ran, ran, ran with her, right up to the top of the ground. Then they said, --

"Poke your head through!"

So she poked her head through, and she was in the midst of a beautiful garden. It was springtime, and all the other flowers had their heads poked through, and she was the prettiest little pink rose in the whole garden!

6. Part A

What is this story about?

Ⓐ Taking the time to do things we like
Ⓑ Good things happen when you take a risk.
Ⓒ Flowers in a garden.
Ⓓ The importance of the sun and the rain.

Part B

What happened in the at the end of the story?

Ⓐ Rosebud hid in the garden.
Ⓑ Rosebud hid in her house.
Ⓒ Rosebud made new friends with Sun and Rain.
Ⓓ Rosebud bloomed into a beautiful rose.

My mother works extremely hard as a nurse. Each day she gives her all, and when she comes home, she is dog tired. I like to help her take a load off, so I try and make dinner for her. I also clean the house and mow the yard outside. Today was even more difficult, though. It rained like cats and dogs all afternoon, so I couldn't take care of the yard. Then, when I came inside to clean, I realized the kitchen sink was clogged, and the washing machine seemed broken. I couldn't catch a break! By the time Mom came home, I had given up, called a plumber, and ordered a pizza. It's a good thing my mom always taught me that where there is a will, there is a way!

7. Why does the author want to help his mother?

Ⓐ She is gone all day.
Ⓑ She works hard as a nurse.
Ⓒ She does not like housework.
Ⓓ She is a new mother.

My cousin lives in California. Because that is such a long distance from Philadelphia, it is not a short drive, so I only see her once a year. This distance makes it so hard to visit her, and I miss her very much.

Our parents think it is too hard to drive across the country to see each other. I want to see her more often so we can see movies together,` but our parents say no!

8. What is this passage about?

Ⓐ The author wants to see her cousin.
Ⓑ The author's parents do not like to drive.
Ⓒ The author's cousin does not like to see movies.
Ⓓ The author wants to move to California.

Challenge Yourself!

- **Multiplication & Division of Powers of Ten**
- **Summarizing Texts**

https://www.lumoslearning.com/a/dc5-5

Day 5

See Page 7 for Signup details

Learn Sign Language

What is American Sign Language?

American Sign Language (ASL) is a complete, complex language that employs signs made by moving the hands combined with facial expressions and postures of the body. It is the primary language of many North Americans who are deaf and is one of several communication options used by people who are deaf or hard-of-hearing.

Where did ASL originate?

The exact beginnings of ASL are not clear, but some suggest that it arose more than 200 years ago from the intermixing of local sign languages and French Sign Language (LSF, or Langue des Signes Française). Today's ASL includes some elements of LSF plus the original local sign languages, which over the years have melded and changed into a rich, complex, and mature language. Modern ASL and modern LSF are distinct languages and, while they still contain some similar signs, can no longer be understood by each other's users.

Source: https://www.nidcd.nih.gov/health/american-sign-language

Why should one learn sign language?

Enrich your cognitive skills: Sign language can enrich the cognitive development of a child. Since, different cognitive skills can be acquired as a child, learning sign language, can be implemented with practice and training in early childhood.

Make new friends: You could communicate better with the hearing-impaired people you meet, if you know the sign language, it is easier to understand and communicate effectively.

Volunteer: Use your ASL skills to interpret as a volunteer. volunteers can help in making a real difference in people's lives, with their time, effort and commitment.

Bilingual: If you are monolingual, here is an opportunity to become bilingual, with a cause.

Private chat: It would be useful to converse with a friend or in a group without anyone understanding, what you are up to.

Let's Learn the Alphabets

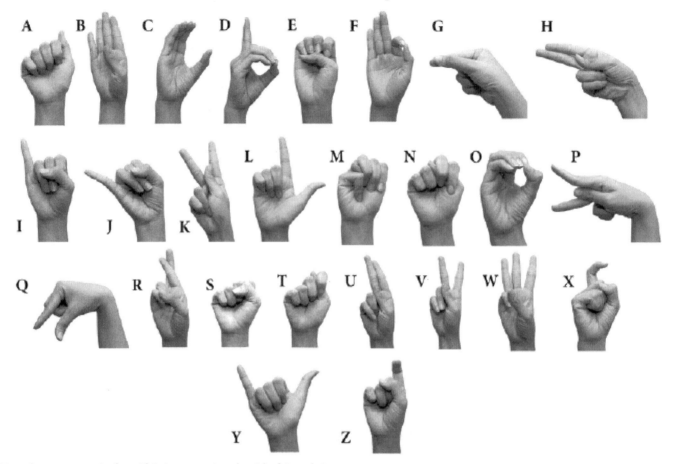

Sign language is fun if it is practiced with friends!
Partner with your friends or family members and try the following activities.

Activity

1. Communicate the following to your friend using the ASL.
   * USA
   * ASL

If your friend hasn't mastered the ASL yet, give the above alphabet chart to your friend.

2. Try saying your name in ASL using the hand gestures.

3. Have your friend communicate a funny word using ASL and you try to read it without the help of the chart. List the words you tried below.

Let's Learn Some Words

RED

ORANGE

YELLOW

GREEN

PURPLE

BLUE

EAT

DRINK

MORE

PLEASE

THANK YOU

SORRY

Let's Learn the Numbers

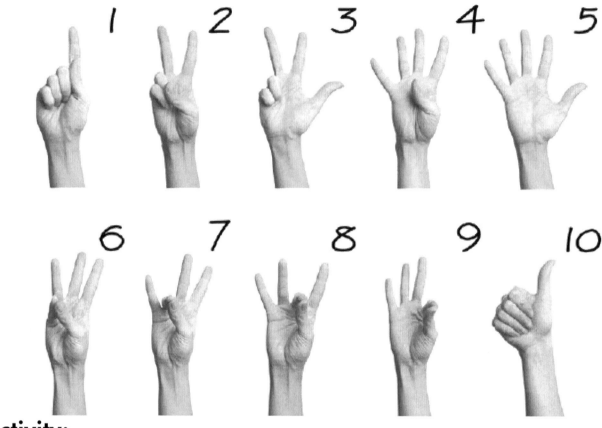

Activity:

1. Share your postal code through ASL to your friend.
2. Communicate your home phone number in ASL to your friend.

This Week's Online Activities

- **Reading Assignment**
- **Vocabulary Practice**
- **Write Your Summer Diary**

https://www.lumoslearning.com/a/slh5-6

See Page 7 for Signup details

Weekly Fun Summer Photo Contest

Take a picture of your summer fun activity and share it on Twitter or Instagram

Use the **#SummerLearning** mention

@LumosLearning on Twitter or

@lumos.learning on Instagram

Tag friends and increase your chances of winning the contest

Participate and stand a chance to WIN $50 Amazon gift card!

Read and Write Decimals (5.NBT.A.3.A)

1.   **How is the number four hundredths written?**

Ⓐ 0.04
Ⓑ 0.400
Ⓒ 400.0
Ⓓ 0.004

2.   **How is the number 0.2 read?**

Ⓐ Zero and two
Ⓑ Decimal two
Ⓒ Two tenths
Ⓓ Two hundredths

3.   **What is the decimal form of $\frac{7}{10}$?**

Ⓐ 7.10
Ⓑ 0.7
Ⓒ 10.7
Ⓓ 0.07

4. **Read the equations below and indicate whether they are true or false.**

	True	False
345.3 = three hundred forty-five and three hundredths.	◯	◯
$900 \times 30 \times 2 \times 4 \times (\frac{1}{10}) \times 7(\frac{1}{100}) >$ Nine hundred thirty-two and four hundredths	◯	◯
$604.2 = 600 \times 4 \times 2 \times (\frac{1}{100})$	◯	◯
1.805 > One and ninety-two hundredths	◯	◯

Salmon

A fish that is a great favorite with people is salmon. It begins its life in a small pool up a river. Far from the sea, the fish lays its eggs in a pool in the river. When the baby fish are a few inches long, they begin to swim down the river. As they grow bigger, they make their way towards the sea.

They jump over rocks, often with their tails first. Suddenly, they find themselves in the sea. The fish live in the sea for three years. They swim far away from land. How do they find their way back? These fish have a wonderful sense of smell. They remember the scent of their journey easily
because the river flowed to the sea and carried them there. After three years, most salmon swim toward the pools.

As soon as they reach a pool, the females lay their eggs. They lay their eggs near the edge of the water and cover them with sand. Soon the eggs hatch, and the pool is full of small fish, getting ready for the long journey out to the sea.

5. What is the first important event that happens in this story?

Ⓐ Salmon are a favorite of many people.
Ⓑ The fish lay their eggs in the river.
Ⓒ The fish live in the ocean for three years.
Ⓓ The fish swim to the ocean.

Do Your Best

Katie stood before the crowd blushing and wringing her hands. She looked out and saw the room full of faces. Some she knew and some she did not. But, they were all here to listen to her. Taking a deep breath, she opened her mouth, but no words came out. Tears formed in the corners of her eyes as she closed them.

With her eyes closed, she imagined her mother helping her get dressed and ready for tonight. "Just do your best," is what her mother had told her. She opened her eyes and found her mother's smiling face in the crowd. Relaxing, she took another deep breath and started singing. She did not stop until she finished, and the crowd was on their feet applauding.

After the show, she found her parents and her friends. They all had wonderful things to say about her song and how proud they were because she kept going even when it seemed like she might give up. She shrugged her shoulders and shared a smile with her mother. "I just did my best," she answered.

6. What happened the second time Katie took a deep breath?

Ⓐ She looked at her mother.
Ⓑ She could not sing.
Ⓒ She sang beautifully.
Ⓓ She cried.

7. Using the letter at the beginning of each sentence, put the sentences into the correct order to make a paragraph.

A. Emily asks her mother to put the pan in the oven.
B. Emily loves to cook.
C. Emily loves brownies.
D. Emily asks her mother if she can make a snack.
E. She mixes the brownie mix, eggs, and oil together and pours them in a pan.

Ⓐ B, C, D, E, A
Ⓑ B, D, C, E, A
Ⓒ A, B, D, E, C
Ⓓ E, C, A, D, B

THE LITTLE PINK ROSE
Best Stories to Tell to Children (1912)
By Sara Cone Bryant

Once there was a little pink Rosebud, and she lived down in a little dark house under the ground. One day she was sitting there, all by herself, and it was very still. Suddenly, she heard a little tap, tap, tap, at the door. "Who is that?" she said.

"It's the Rain, and I want to come in," said a soft, sad, little voice.

"No, you can't come in," said the little Rosebud. Then it was very still for a long time. At last, there came a little rustling, whispering sound, all around the window: rustle, whisper, whisper. "Who is there?" said the little Rosebud.

"It's the Sunshine," said a little, soft, cheery voice, "and I want to come in!"

"N -- no," said the little pink rose, "you can't come in." And she sat still again.

Pretty soon, she heard the sweet little rustling noise at the key-hole. "Who is there?" she said.

"It's the Sunshine," said the cheery little voice, "and I want to come in. I want to come in!"
"No, no," said the little pink rose, "you cannot come in."

By and by, as she sat so still, she heard tap, tap, tap, and rustle, whisper, rustle, all up and down the windowpane, and on the door, and at the key-hole. "Who is there?" she said.

"It's the Rain and the Sun, the Rain and the Sun," said two little voices, together, "and we want to come in! We want to come in! We want to come in!"

"Dear, dear," said the little Rosebud, "if there are two of you, I s'pose I shall have to let you in." So she opened the door a little wee crack, and they came in. And one took one of her little hands, and the other took her other little hand, and they ran, ran, ran with her, right up to the top of the ground. Then they said, --"Poke your head through!"

So she poked her head through, and she was in the midst of a beautiful garden. It was springtime, and all the other flowers had their heads poked through, and she was the prettiest little pink rose in the whole garden!

8. **Sequence the events in the proper order so that they form the correct timeline of the story. Enter your answers in correct sequence in the boxes given below**

   Ⓐ A. Rosebud poked her head above ground.
   Ⓑ B. Rosebud heard a strange sound
   Ⓒ C. Rosebud let her visitors in;
   Ⓓ D. Rosebud had visitors;

   ╭───╮
   ╰───╯

   ╭───╮
   ╰───╯

   ╭───╮
   ╰───╯

   ╭───╮
   ╰───╯

Challenge Yourself!

- **Read and Write Decimals**
- **Events**

https://www.lumoslearning.com/a/dc5-6

See Page 7 for Signup details

Day 1

1. Which of the following numbers is the least?
   0.04, 4.00, 0.40, 40.0

   Ⓐ 0.04
   Ⓑ 4.00
   Ⓒ 0.40
   Ⓓ 40.0

2. Which of the following numbers is greatest?
   0.125, 0.251, 0.512, 0.215

   Ⓐ 0.125
   Ⓑ 0.251
   Ⓒ 0.512
   Ⓓ 0.215

3. Which of the following numbers is less than seven hundredths?

   Ⓐ 0.072
   Ⓑ 0.60
   Ⓒ 0.058
   Ⓓ All of these

4. Order the following numbers from least to greatest.

   1.003, 0.853, 0.85, 1.03, 0.96, 0.921

   Enter your answers in the correct order in the box given below

Day 2

A Clever Idea

Once there was a severe drought. There was little water in Tony's well, and he didn't know what would happen to the fruit trees in his garden. Just then, he noticed three men looking intently at his house. He was certain that the three strangers were planning to rob his house. He acted quickly. He shouted out to his son, "My son, due to the drought, money has become scarce. There are many thieves. Let us protect our valuables, and put all of our jewels in a box and throw them into the well. They will be safe there." He quickly told his son to put some large stones in a box and throw them into the well.

The thieves heard the sound of the box falling into the well and were happy. That night they came to the well. The box was heavy and had landed deep down in the well. To get it, they would have to take out some of the water. They started drawing water from the well and pouring it onto the ground. Tony had made arrangements to make sure that the water reached his fruit trees. He had channels leading from the well to each of the trees. By the time thieves found the box, they had drawn out enough water to water the trees. It was almost dawn. Tony sent for the soldiers, and just as the thieves were trying to open the box, they were caught red-handed.

5. What is the setting of the story?

- Ⓐ It takes place in the countryside.
- Ⓑ It takes place in Tony's backyard.
- Ⓒ Both A and B
- Ⓓ None of the above

6. Which detail in the above story tells us that this story possibly took place during the past?

- Ⓐ "Tony sent for the soldiers, and just as the thieves were trying to open the box, they were caught red-handed."
- Ⓑ "Once there was a severe drought."
- Ⓒ He shouted out to his son, "My son, due to the drought, money has become scarce."
- Ⓓ "By the time the thieves found the box, they had drawn out enough water to water the trees."

THE LITTLE PINK ROSE
Best Stories to Tell to Children (1912)
By Sara Cone Bryant

Once there was a little pink Rosebud, and she lived down in a little dark house under the ground. One day she was sitting there, all by herself, and it was very still. Suddenly, she heard a little tap, tap, tap, at the door. "Who is that?" she said.

"It's the Rain, and I want to come in," said a soft, sad, little voice.

"No, you can't come in," the little Rosebud said. By and by she heard another little tap, tap, tap, on the Donpane. "Who is there?" she said.

The same soft little voice answered, "It's the Rain, and I want to come in!"

"No, you can't come in," said the little Rosebud. Then it was very still for a long time. At last, there came a little rustling, whispering sound, all around the window: rustle, whisper, whisper. "Who is there?" said the little Rosebud.

"It's the Sunshine," said a little, soft, cheery voice, "and I want to come in!"

"N -- no," said the little pink rose, "you can't come in." And she sat still again.

Pretty soon, she heard the sweet little rustling noise at the key-hole. "Who is there?" she said.

"It's the Sunshine," said the cheery little voice, "and I want to come in. I want to come in!"

"No, no," said the little pink rose, "you cannot come in."

By and by, as she sat so still, she heard tap, tap, tap, and rustle, whisper, rustle, all up and down the windowpane, and on the door, and at the key-hole. "Who is there?" she said.

"It's the Rain and the Sun, the Rain and the Sun," said two little voices, together, "and we want to come in! We want to come in! We want to come in!"

"Dear, dear," said the little Rosebud, "if there are two of you, I s'pose I shall have to let you in." So she opened the door a little wee crack, and they came in. And one took one of her little hands, and the other took her other little hand, and they ran, ran, ran with her, right up to the top of the ground. Then they said, --

"Poke your head through!"

So she poked her head through, and she was in the midst of a beautiful garden. It was springtime, and all the other flowers had their heads poked through, and she was the prettiest little pink rose in the whole garden!

7. Part A

What is the main setting of the above story?

Ⓐ In a garden
Ⓑ In a forest
Ⓒ In a town
Ⓓ In a zoo

7. Part B

Which sentence indicates that the majority of the story takes place below ground?

Ⓐ So she opened the door a little wee crack, and they came in.
Ⓑ She was the prettiest little pink rose in the whole garden!
Ⓒ By and by, as she sat so still, she heard tap, tap, tap, and rustle, whisper, rustle, all up and down the windowpane, and on the door, and at the key-hole.
Ⓓ And one took one of her little hands, and the other took her other little hand, and they ran, ran, ran with her, right up to the top of the ground.

8. If a setting is important to the story, it is usually established _____.

Ⓐ at the end.
Ⓑ at the beginning.
Ⓒ in the middle
Ⓓ only by illustrations

Challenge Yourself!

- **Comparing & Ordering Decimals**
- **Setting**

https://www.lumoslearning.com/a/dc5-7

Day 2

See Page 7 for Signup details

1.   **Is $7.48 closest to $6, $7 or $8?**

    Ⓐ $6
    Ⓑ $7
    Ⓒ $8
    Ⓓ It is right in the middle of $7 and $8

2.   **Round the Olympic time of 56.389 seconds to the nearest tenth of a second.**

    Ⓐ 56.0
    Ⓑ 57
    Ⓒ 56.4
    Ⓓ 56.39

3.   **Round the number 57.81492 to the nearest hundredth.**

    Ⓐ 57.82
    Ⓑ 58.00
    Ⓒ 57.80
    Ⓓ 57.81

4. **Read each statement below and mark the correct column to indicate whether you must round up or keep the digit.**

	Round Up	Keep
Round 5.483 to the nearest hundredth.	◯	◯
Round 6.625 to the nearest tenth.	◯	◯
Round 77.951 to the nearest one.	◯	◯
Round 172.648 to the nearest hundredth.	◯	◯

Day 3

My daddy is a tiger
My mother is a bear
My sister is a pest
Who messes with my hair
And even though my home
Is like living in a zoo
I know my family loves me
And will take care of me too

5. How many similes are in the poem above?

Ⓐ One
Ⓑ Two
Ⓒ Three
Ⓓ Four

6. How many metaphors are in the poem above?

Ⓐ One
Ⓑ Two
Ⓒ Three
Ⓓ Four

My mother is very particular about giving me healthy food. I only eat French fries once in a blue moon.

7. The expression, once in a blue moon, is an example of _____ .

Ⓐ an idiom
Ⓑ a simile
Ⓒ a metaphor
Ⓓ none of the above

8. Read each sentence and match it to the correct figure of speech

	a simile	personification	metaphor
The sea glittered like diamonds under the harsh sun rays.	○	○	○
The spoon ran away to find a better home.	○	○	○
The pillow was as soft as cotton.	○	○	○
The biscuit was a paper weight.	○	○	○

Challenge Yourself!

- **Rounding Decimals**
- **Figurative Language**

https://www.lumoslearning.com/a/dc5-8

See Page 7 for Signup details

Day 3

Day 4

1.   Solve. 79 x 14

     Ⓐ 790
     Ⓑ 1,106
     Ⓒ 854
     Ⓓ 224

2.   A farmer plants 18 rows of beans. If there are 50 bean plants in each row, how many plants will he have altogether?

     Ⓐ 908
     Ⓑ 68
     Ⓒ 900
     Ⓓ 98

3.   Solve. 680 x 94 = _____

     Ⓐ 64,070
     Ⓑ 63,960
     Ⓒ 64,760
     Ⓓ 63,920

4. What is the product of 321 X 1854
Enter your answer in the box given below.

The Orange

Even though no one knows exactly where oranges come from, Southeast Asia is believed to be their first home. They are grown today in most of the warmer parts of the world. The ancient Greeks and Romans knew about oranges. It is possible that oranges were carried from India to Western Asia and then to Europe.

The Spaniards took the sour oranges to the West Indies and from there to Florida, in America. Today, oranges are the most important fresh fruit in international trade. There are three different kinds of oranges: the sweet or common orange, the mandarin orange, and the sour or bitter orange.

One type of sweet orange is called the blood orange. It has a pulp with a deep red color. This type of orange is grown mostly in the Mediterranean region. Mandarin oranges are mainly found in Florida. Sour oranges are grown almost everywhere, with Spain having the greatest number used for trade. These sour oranges are generally used to make marmalade.

However, they can be put to many other interesting uses, from making medicine to creating perfumes. Oranges have many medicinal values. Oranges are the fruit with the greatest concentration of vitamin C. The skin of the orange helps to keep the fruit inside from becoming damaged and to remain clean. The thick, oily, and bitter skin does not allow any insects to get into an orange. Many kinds of useful oils can be extracted from the thick skin. Oranges are healthy and delicious.

5. Where can you find the conclusion of this passage?

Ⓐ At the beginning of the passage.
Ⓑ In the middle of the passage.
Ⓒ At the end of the passage.
Ⓓ A passage never has an ending.

What is this life if, full of care,
We have no time to stand and stare?

No time to stand beneath the boughs
And stare as long as sheep or cows.

No time to see, when woods we pass,
Where squirrels hide their nuts in grass

No time to see, in broad daylight,
Streams full of stars, like skies at night.

No time to turn at Beauty's glance,
And watch her feet, how they can dance.

No time to wait till her mouth can
 Enrich that smile her eyes began.'

A poor life if, full of care,
We have no time to stand and stare

-- W. H. Davies

6. What is the first stanza of the poem doing?

Ⓐ Asking a question.
Ⓑ Answering a question.
Ⓒ Introducing life.
Ⓓ Introducing the poet.

7. Who wrote this poem?

Ⓐ An unknown poet
Ⓑ W. H. Davies
Ⓒ Life
Ⓓ No one

8. When you read a humorous piece of writing, you usually _____.

Ⓐ cry
Ⓑ become serious
Ⓒ write down information
Ⓓ laugh

Challenge Yourself!

- **Multiplication of Whole Numbers**
- **Structures of Text**

https://www.lumoslearning.com/a/dc5-9

Day 4

See Page 7 for Signup details

Day 5

1. Find the missing number:

48 ÷ ___ = 12

Ⓐ 4
Ⓑ 10
Ⓒ 6
Ⓓ 8

2. Hannah is filling gift bags for a party. She has 72 pieces of candy to pass out. If there are 8 bags, how many pieces of candy will go in each bag?

Ⓐ 8
Ⓑ 10
Ⓒ 9
Ⓓ 7

3. Solve. 1,248 ÷ 6

Ⓐ 2,080
Ⓑ 208
Ⓒ 28
Ⓓ 280

4. Which of the following completes the equation 564 ÷ _____ = 47
Circle the correct answer choice

Ⓐ 13
Ⓑ 18
Ⓒ 12
Ⓓ 28

Day 5

Late for School

Marrah heard the brakes on the bus as she shoveled the rest of her breakfast into her mouth. "You just missed the bus!" Marrah's mother yelled. "Why can't you ever be on time?"

"I'm sorry, Mom," Marrah sighed. She ran upstairs to her room so she could get her backpack, knowing she needed to hurry because her mother would have to take her to school.

"Let's go, Marrah!" Her mother called from downstairs. "You don't want to be late for school too!"

Frantic now, Marrah lifted her sheets to look under them before dropping to her knees in front of her bed. She pushed mounds of clothes out of the way as she continued to search for her backpack.

"Marrah!" Her mother called again. She could hear the impatience in her mother's voice downstairs. She ran out of her room and leaned over the rail.

"I can't find my backpack!" She cried out.

"You mean this one?" Her mother pulled the bag from the floor beside her.

"Oh," she replied, her shoulders sagging as she walked down the stairs.

"Let's go to school, Marrah." Her mother said with a small smile on her face as they walked out the door.

5. How might this story be different if the author told it from the point of view of Marrah's mother?

Ⓐ The story would have described Marrah's frustration.
Ⓑ The story would not change.
Ⓒ The story would describe her mother's frustration.
Ⓓ The story would focus on the bus driver's experience.

The first person point of view _____.

6. Select the phrase that best completes the above sentence.

Ⓐ has the character tell the story in his own words and uses the word "I".
Ⓑ has the character tell the story in his own words and uses pronouns like "he" and "she."
Ⓒ has the ability to show what is happening in many places but does not reveal the thoughts of the characters.
Ⓓ has the narrator tell the story to another character using the pronoun "you."

THE LITTLE PINK ROSE
Best Stories to Tell to Children (1912)
By Sara Cone Bryant

Once there was a little pink Rosebud, and she lived down in a little dark house under the ground. One day she was sitting there, all by herself, and it was very still. Suddenly, she heard a little tap, tap, tap, at the door. "Who is that?" she said.

"It's the Rain, and I want to come in," said a soft, sad, little voice.

"No, you can't come in," the little Rosebud said. By and by she heard another little tap, tap, tap, on the windowpane. "Who is there?" she said.

The same soft little voice answered, "It's the Rain, and I want to come in!"

"No, you can't come in," said the little Rosebud. Then it was very still for a long time. At last, there came a little rustling, whispering sound, all around the window: rustle, whisper, whisper. "Who is there?" said the little Rosebud.

"It's the Sunshine," said a little, soft, cheery voice, "and I want to come in!"

"N -- no," said the little pink rose, "you can't come in." And she sat still again.

Pretty soon, she heard the sweet little rustling noise at the key-hole. "Who is there?" she said.

"It's the Sunshine," said the cheery little voice, "and I want to come in. I want to come in!"

"No, no," said the little pink rose, "you cannot come in."

By and by, as she sat so still, she heard tap, tap, tap, and rustle, whisper, rustle, all up and down the windowpane, and on the door, and at the key-hole. "Who is there?" she said.

"It's the Rain and the Sun, the Rain and the Sun," said two little voices, together, "and we want to come in! We want to come in! We want to come in!"

"Dear, dear," said the little Rosebud, "if there are two of you, I s'pose I shall have to let you in." So she opened the door a little wee crack, and they came in. And one took one of her little hands, and the other took her other little hand, and they ran, ran, ran with her, right up to the top of the ground. Then they said, --
"Poke your head through!"

So she poked her head through, and she was in the midst of a beautiful garden. It was springtime, and all the other flowers had their heads poked through, and she was the prettiest little pink rose in the whole garden!

7. How might this story be different if it were told from the point of view of the sun?

[blank answer box]

8. Read each sentence and match it to the point of view from which it is being told.

	First Person	Third Person
While we were walking together, I lost my dog.	○	○
Kelsey was extremely upset. While she and Danny were together, he got lost.	○	○
This is the first time we have had a chance to go to the zoo.	○	○

Challenge Yourself!

- **Division of Whole Numbers**
- **Styles of Narration**

https://www.lumoslearning.com/a/dc5-10

Day 5

See Page 7 for Signup details

7 Techniques to Improve Your Coloring/Painting Skills

Have you ever thought, "I wish I could paint like that" as you walked through the museum or flipped through pages of a book?

Is the inner artist inside you waiting to be awakened? Dying to express your imagination, creativity, and artistic talent, but you do not know where to start.

Well, wait no more below are some tips that can help you showcase and improve the inner artist in you:

1. Get to know art

If you are passionate about being a painter and want to be taken seriously, then put effort into understanding art.

Read art books, study famous paintings and their significance, visit museums, and get to know art. Research to learn the basics: the medium that you are interested in, the basics of the color wheel, and different types of art available.

2. Choose a medium that you like

Now that you have foundational knowledge about art, narrow your interests.

Although each of us an inner artist inside, it's easier to perfect the craft if you are focused on a medium that sparks your interest the most.

This saves your time and allows more opportunity for you to cultivate and develop your newfound skill.

3. Get the supplies you'll need

This can become very costly, depending on the amount of supplies you want to have: for painting, you'll need different types of brushes, various paints, diverse set of canvasses.

I suggest starting with the basics; a starter set brush pack, a basic selection of color paints, you can always mix various colors to get another desired effect or shade.

On sale, art supplies are always a good starter to experiment with.

4. The tryout stage

This is the true "self-expression" period. It is during this time that you experiment with your supplies and preferences.

Try mixing different colors; dark mixed with light colors, the amount of ratio needed when you're mixing 2 or 3 colors depending on the desired effect. Do you want a lighter or darker shade? It's also a good idea to practice different strokes of the brushes. Softer strokes give you lighter effects while the harder, more forceful strokes most likely will turn out darker.

This will be the time where you will discover your strengths and weaknesses in painting or coloring.

5. Reach out to other artists like you

Ask for advice and tips from other artists like you. Learn from their experience. Get their opinion on different types of painting materials, brand preferences based on previous work experience.

If you are up for it, show them your work. Welcome constructive feedback, as a developing artist, the best way to improve your skills is by receiving honest, constructive pointers.

6. Develop your own signature style

Now that you've gotten the basics of painting/coloring, its time for you to develop your own style.

Surely, there are too many to count impressive artists that we all look up to and emulate. But developing your own style is important and makes you more unforgettable.

Do you paint abstracts only; do you like creating portraits or landscapes? Regardless of what you choose, its ideal to have that signature style.

7. Think and see the world as an artist

Now that you've mastered the basics, did your homework by studying, crafted your signature style, and finally created a few masterpieces.

Start looking at the world from an artist's point of view, see the world in the eyes of an artist. Look for opportunities to give you ideas and to express yourself through painting. Observe the light, the intensity of the shade of the moon, and the color schemes that flowers may have. Take notice of the body language that people have when they're interacting with one another and translate those emotions into a canvas.

So go ahead express your feelings through a painting, who knows your work of art might be the next one featured in that museum or book that you once admired.

This Week's Online Activities

- **Reading Assignment**
- **Vocabulary Practice**
- **Write Your Summer Diary**

https://www.lumoslearning.com/a/slh5-6

See Page 7 for Signup details

Weekly Fun Summer Photo Contest

📷 Take a picture of your summer fun activity and share it on Twitter or Instagram

Use the **#SummerLearning** mention

@LumosLearning on Twitter 🐦 or

@lumos.learning on Instagram 📷

◀ Tag friends and increase your chances of winning the contest

Participate and stand a chance to WIN $50 Amazon gift card!

Week 3 Summer Practice

Add, Subtract, Multiply, and Divide Decimals (5.NBT.B.7)

Day 1

1. At a math competition, three members of a team each solved a problem as quickly as they could. Their times were 4.18 seconds, 3.75 seconds, and 3.99 seconds. What was the total of their times?

    Ⓐ 11.92 seconds
    Ⓑ 10.99 seconds
    Ⓒ 10.72 seconds
    Ⓓ 11.72 seconds

2. Beginning with the number 6.472, add:
    1 hundredth
    3 ones
    5 tenths
    What is the result?

    Ⓐ 7.822
    Ⓑ 6.823
    Ⓒ 9.982
    Ⓓ 6.607

3. Find the perimeter (total length of all four sides) of a trapezoid whose sides measure 2.09 ft, 2.09 ft, 3.72 ft, and 6.60 ft.

    Ⓐ 16.12 ft
    Ⓑ 14.5 ft
    Ⓒ 13.50 ft
    Ⓓ 8.56 ft

4. Solve:
   0.05 ÷ 0.2
   Enter your answer in the box below.

   _____

Day 1

Eliza stood beside the winding train. It seemed to go on for miles and miles! The noise was unbearable at times, and she was constantly dirty. Ma and Pa told her that this would not be a fun way to travel, but she was so excited to go that she said she did not care. Now, all that Eliza can think of is a clean bed and a quiet rest.

5. Select the phrase that best completes the below sentence.

Without the added image, the reader might _____.

   Ⓐ think Eliza is describing a car ride.
   Ⓑ think Eliza is describing an actual train ride.
   Ⓒ believe the author is confused.
   Ⓓ think the author needs more details.

6. What is media in relation to text?

   Ⓐ Media uses sounds, images, and language.
   Ⓑ Media uses sounds, movies, and language.
   Ⓒ Media uses sounds, verbs, and metaphors.
   Ⓓ Media uses sounds, similes, and alliteration.

Tommy cannot decide what sort of top he should wear. Closing his eyes, he imagines all of the different ones he has.

7. Part A

Select the phrase that best completes the above sentence.
The picture adds additional information to the text because it _____.

Ⓐ helps visual learners.
Ⓑ defines the top as a shirt that he would like to wear.
Ⓒ does not add any information.
Ⓓ defines the top as a type of hat.

Part B
Select the phrase that best completes the above sentence.
Without the added image, the reader might assume _____.

Ⓐ that Tommy is talking about shirts.
Ⓑ that the author is confused.
Ⓒ that Tommy is confused.
Ⓓ that Tommy is playing a game.

8. Which visual aide works best in informational text?

Ⓐ Internet link
Ⓑ illustration
Ⓒ text only
Ⓓ bar graph

Challenge Yourself!

- **Add, Subtract, Multiply, and Divide Decimals**
- **Visual Elements**

https://www.lumoslearning.com/a/dc5-11

Day 1

See Page 7 for Signup details

1. Add: $\dfrac{2}{10} + \dfrac{1}{10} =$

    (A) $\dfrac{3}{20}$

    (B) $\dfrac{3}{10}$

    (C) $\dfrac{1}{10}$

    (D) $\dfrac{2}{10}$

2. To make a bowl of punch, Joe mixed $1\dfrac{1}{4}$ gallons of juice with $1\dfrac{2}{4}$ gallons of sparkling water. How much punch does he have?

    (A) $2\dfrac{3}{4}$ gallons

    (B) 3 gallons

    (C) $\dfrac{1}{4}$ gallon

    (D) $\dfrac{3}{4}$ gallon

3. Subtract: $\dfrac{3}{4} - \dfrac{2}{4} =$

    (A) $\dfrac{5}{4}$

    (B) $\dfrac{1}{4}$

    (C) $\dfrac{3}{4}$

    (D) 1

4. What is the value of $\dfrac{3}{5} - \dfrac{2}{7}$

    Write your answer in the box given below.

What is this life if, full of care,
We have no time to stand and stare?

No time to stand beneath the boughs
And stare as long as sheep or cows.

No time to see, when woods we pass,
Where squirrels hide their nuts in grass

No time to see, in broad daylight,
Streams full of stars, like skies at night.

No time to turn at Beauty's glance,
And watch her feet, how they can dance.

No time to wait till her mouth can
Enrich that smile her eyes began.

A poor life if, full of care,
We have no time to stand and stare.
-- W. H. Davies

In the kitchen,
After the aimless
Chatter of the plates,
The murmur of the stoves,
The chuckles of the water pipes,
And the sharp exchanges
Of the knives, forks, and spoons,
Comes the serious quiet
When the sink slowly clears its throat,
And you can hear the occasional rumble
Of the refrigerator's tummy
As it digests the cold.

5. How are these two poems similar?

    Ⓐ Both poems use similes.
    Ⓑ Both poems use personification.
    Ⓒ Both poems use colorful descriptions.
    Ⓓ Both poems use metaphors.

6. What things might you look for when comparing two pieces of text?

  Ⓐ type of text
  Ⓑ purpose of text
  Ⓒ style of text
  Ⓓ all of the above

Number of library books borrowed in 2016	
Month	Number of books borrowed
September	660
October	670
November	570
December	475

7. From the above table, which two months had the largest number of library books borrowed?

  Ⓐ September and December
  Ⓑ September and October
  Ⓒ October and November
  Ⓓ October and December

8. Refer to the chart above to complete the sentence below.
Students borrowed the least number of books in _____ 2016.

  Ⓐ November
  Ⓑ October
  Ⓒ September
  Ⓓ December

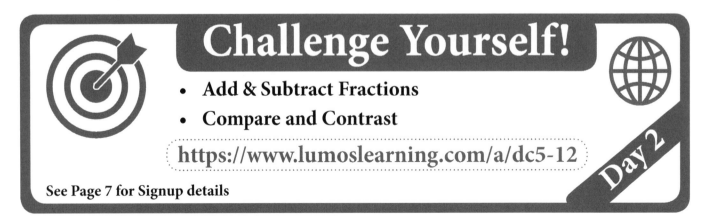

Challenge Yourself!

- Add & Subtract Fractions
- Compare and Contrast

https://www.lumoslearning.com/a/dc5-12

Day 2

See Page 7 for Signup details

Day 3

1. Susan's homework was to practice the piano for 3/4 of an hour each night. How many minutes each night did she practice?

    Ⓐ 30 minutes
    Ⓑ 15 minutes
    Ⓒ 45 minutes
    Ⓓ 60 minutes

2. Three fifths of the 30 students are boys. How many students are girls?

    Ⓐ 12 girls
    Ⓑ 18 girls
    Ⓒ 6 girls
    Ⓓ 8 girls

3. Walking at a steady pace, Ella walked 11 miles in 3 hours. Which mixed number shows how many miles she walked in an hour?

    Ⓐ $\dfrac{2}{3}$
    Ⓑ $2\dfrac{2}{3}$
    Ⓒ 3
    Ⓓ $3\dfrac{2}{3}$

4. Match the statement with the symbol that will make the statement true

			>	<	=
$\dfrac{5}{6} - \dfrac{2}{3}$	☐	$\dfrac{1}{2} - \dfrac{3}{8}$	◯	◯	◯
$\dfrac{5}{6} + \dfrac{2}{3}$	☐	$\dfrac{3}{4} + \dfrac{5}{12}$	◯	◯	◯
$\dfrac{3}{15} + \dfrac{2}{5}$	☐	$\dfrac{1}{3} + \dfrac{2}{5}$	◯	◯	◯
$\dfrac{7}{8} - \dfrac{1}{4}$	☐	$\dfrac{3}{4} - \dfrac{1}{8}$	◯	◯	◯

Mrs. Davis lived in a great big apartment on the top floor of her building. As the doctor walked into her spacious, clean apartment, he noticed fine, leather furniture and expensive works of art. Mrs. Davis sat up in her large, king-sized bed wearing a beautiful, silk robe. Dr. Thomas took Mrs. Davis's temperature and listened to her heart. "You seem to be feeling better this afternoon, Mrs. Davis," commented the doctor.

5. What can you infer about Mrs. Davis after reading the passage above?

Ⓐ Mrs. Davis is a wealthy woman.
Ⓑ Mrs. Davis is an intelligent woman.
Ⓒ Mrs. Davis is a beautiful woman.
Ⓓ Mrs. Davis is a young woman.

6. After reading the paragraph above, what can you infer about the reason for Dr. Thomas's visit?

Ⓐ Dr. Thomas is visiting Mrs. Davis, because she was sick.
Ⓑ Dr. Thomas is visiting Mrs. Davis, because he is her new neighbor.
Ⓒ Dr. Thomas is visiting Mrs. Davis, because he needs a favor.
Ⓓ Dr. Thomas is visiting Mrs. Davis, because it is her birthday.

7. Select the phrase that best completes the sentence.

Kara's mother wakes up at 5:30 A.M. every morning so she'll have time to study for her college classes. This is the only time she has to study before she has to go to work. She takes college classes two nights a week. Every weekend, she volunteers at the local homeless shelter. She has been helping out there for the past three years.

From the information in the paragraph above, one can infer that Kara's mother is probably _____.

Ⓐ married to a college professor
Ⓑ a very hard-working woman
Ⓒ tired of going to college
Ⓓ None of the above

8. What do you think "read between the lines" means?
   Circle the correct answer choice

Authors help readers make inferences by giving certain details. However, authors expect readers to "read between the lines."

Ⓐ Figure out what text means.
Ⓑ Look for evidence in text to make inferences.
Ⓒ Come up with ideas or opinions of your own based on what you read.
Ⓓ All of the above

Challenge Yourself!

- **Problem Solving with Fractions**
- **Inferences and Conclusions**

https://www.lumoslearning.com/a/dc5-13

Day 3

See Page 7 for Signup details

Day 4

1. Suppose three friends wanted to share four cookies equally. How many cookies would each friend receive?

   Ⓐ $1\frac{1}{3}$

   Ⓑ $\frac{3}{4}$

   Ⓒ $1\frac{3}{4}$

   Ⓓ $\frac{1}{3}$

2. If 18 is divided by 5, which fraction represents the remainder divided by divisor?

   Ⓐ $\frac{3}{10}$

   Ⓑ $\frac{3}{5}$

   Ⓒ $\frac{5}{10}$

   Ⓓ $\frac{1}{3}$

3. If there are 90 minutes in a soccer game and 4 squads of players will share this time equally, how many minutes will each squad play?

   Ⓐ $\frac{22}{4}$

   Ⓑ $22\frac{1}{2}$

   Ⓒ $22\frac{2}{10}$

   Ⓓ $16\frac{4}{22}$

4. Justine found 6-feet of string with which to make 8 bracelets. If each bracelet was the same length, how long was each bracelet? Enter your answer in the box as a fraction in its simplest form.

Day 4

The Orange

Even though no one knows exactly where oranges come from, Southeast Asia is believed to be their first home. They are grown today in most of the warmer parts of the world. The ancient Greeks and Romans knew about oranges. It is possible that oranges were carried from India to Western Asia and then to Europe.

The Spaniards took the sour oranges to the West Indies and from there to Florida, in America. Today, oranges are the most important fresh fruit in international trade. There are three different kinds of oranges: the sweet or common orange, the mandarin orange, and the sour or bitter orange.

One type of sweet orange is called the blood orange. It has a pulp with a deep red color. This type of orange is grown mostly in the Mediterranean region. Mandarin oranges are mainly found in Florida. Sour oranges are grown almost everywhere, with Spain having the greatest number used for trade. These sour oranges are generally used to make marmalade.

However, they can be put to many other interesting uses, from making medicine to creating perfumes. Oranges have many medicinal values. Oranges are the fruit with the greatest concentration of vitamin C. The skin of the orange helps to keep the fruit inside from becoming damaged and to remain clean. The thick, oily, and bitter skin does not allow any insects to get into an orange. Many kinds of useful oils can be extracted from the thick skin. Oranges are healthy and delicious.

5. What is the author saying about oranges in the first paragraph?

Ⓐ The author is explaining how oranges have been dispersed around the world.
Ⓑ The author is explaining how the ancient Romans and Greeks knew about oranges.
Ⓒ The author is explaining how oranges are traded around the world.
Ⓓ None of the above

6. From your understanding of the above passage, oranges are grown in ___.

Ⓐ Spain
Ⓑ the West Indies
Ⓒ most of the colder parts of the word.
Ⓓ most of the warmer parts of the world.

7. Which detail in the above passage supports the fact that the orange is a clean fruit?

Ⓐ Anyone touching it only touches the outer covering, which is easily taken off.
Ⓑ The thick, oily, and bitter skin does not allow insects to get into the orange.
Ⓒ Both A and B
Ⓓ None, because the orange is a very messy fruit.

8. The second paragraph tells us _____.

Ⓐ about the types of oranges
Ⓑ about where the oranges are grown
Ⓒ about the usefulness of oranges
Ⓓ All of the above

Challenge Yourself!

- **Interpreting Fractions**
- **Main Idea and Supporting Details**

https://www.lumoslearning.com/a/dc5-14

Day 4

See Page 7 for Signup details

1. Multiply: $\dfrac{2}{3}$ x $\dfrac{4}{5}$ =

    Ⓐ $\dfrac{8}{15}$

    Ⓑ $\dfrac{3}{4}$

    Ⓒ $\dfrac{6}{8}$

    Ⓓ $\dfrac{4}{15}$

2. Find the product: 5 x $\dfrac{2}{3}$ x $\dfrac{1}{2}$ =

    Ⓐ $1\dfrac{1}{3}$

    Ⓑ 5

    Ⓒ $2\dfrac{2}{3}$

    Ⓓ $1\dfrac{2}{3}$

3. Which of the following is equivalent to 5/6 x 7?

    Ⓐ $5 \div (6 \times 7)$
    Ⓑ $(5 \times 7) \div 6$
    Ⓒ $(6 \times 7) \div 5$
    Ⓓ $(1 \div 7) \times (5 \div 6)$

4. Fill in the table to complete the math sentence.

$\dfrac{1}{6}$	×		=	$\dfrac{3}{24}$	=	

Day 5

The Glass Cupboard

There was a king who had a cupboard that was made entirely of glass. It was a special cupboard. It looked empty, but you could always take out anything you wanted. There was only one thing you had to remember. Whenever you took something out of it, you had to put something else back in, although nobody knew why.

One day some thieves broke into the palace and stole the cupboard. "Now, we can have anything we want," they said. One of the thieves said, "I want a large bag of gold," and he opened the glass cupboard and got it. The other two did the same, and they, too, got exactly what they wanted. The thieves forgot one thing. Not one of them put anything back in the cupboard.

They went on and on for weeks and months. At last, the leader of the thieves could bear it no longer. He took a hammer and smashed the glass cupboard into a million pieces, and then all three fell dead.

When the king returned home, he ordered his servants to search for the cupboard. When they found it and the dead thieves, they filled sixty great carts with the gold and took it back to the king. He said, "If those thieves had only put something back into the cupboard, they would be alive this day."

He ordered his servants to collect all the pieces of glass and melt into a globe of the world with all the countries on it, and this was to remind himself and others, to give back something in return when someone shows an act of kindness or gives us something

5. What happened when the king was away?

Ⓐ There was a storm, and it smashed the glass cupboard.
Ⓑ The palace servants accidentally broke the glass cupboard.
Ⓒ Some thieves broke into the palace and stole the glass cupboard.
Ⓓ None of the above

6. The reason that the king wanted a globe with all the countries of the world upon it was _____.

Ⓐ to sell it so he could afford to buy a new glass cupboard
Ⓑ to remind himself to give back something when someone gives him something
Ⓒ to remember the thieves that stole the glass cupboard
Ⓓ to prevent thieves from stealing from the palace

Do Your Best

Katie stood before the crowd blushing and wringing her hands. She looked out and saw the room full of faces. Some she knew and some she did not, but they were all here to listen to her. Taking a deep breath, she opened her mouth, but no words came out. Tears formed in the corners of her eyes as she closed them.

With her eyes closed, she imagined her mother helping her get dressed and ready for tonight.

"Just do your best," is what her mother had told her.

She opened her eyes and found her mother's smiling face in the crowd. Relaxing, she took another deep breath and started singing. She did not stop until she finished, and the crowd was on their feet applauding.

After the show, she found her parents and her friends. They all had wonderful things to say about her song and how proud they were because she kept going even when it seemed like she might give up. She shrugged her shoulders and shared a smile with her mother.

"I just did my best," she answered.

7. Part A
What happened when Katie closed her eyes and remembered what her mother had told her?

Ⓐ   She blushed and wringed her hands.
Ⓑ   She started crying and ran off the stage.
Ⓒ   She relaxed and started singing.
Ⓓ   None of the above

Part B
What happened as a result of Katie's singing performance?

Ⓐ   Katie gave up, because she couldn't keep going.
Ⓑ   Her parents and friends told her they were proud of her.
Ⓒ   Her mother helped her get dressed and ready.
Ⓓ   None of the above

Late for School

Marrah heard the air in the bus brakes as she shoveled the rest of her breakfast into her mouth.

"You just missed the bus!" Marrah's mother yelled. "Why can't you ever be on time?"

"I'm sorry, Mom," Marrah sighed. She ran upstairs to her room so she could get her backpack, knowing she needed to hurry because her mother would have to take her to school.

"Let's go, Marrah!" Her mother called from downstairs. "You don't want to be late to school, too!"

Frantic now, Marrah lifted her sheets to look under them before dropping to her knees in front of her bed. She pushed mounds of clothes out of the way as she continued to search for her backpack.

"Marrah!" Her mother called again, and she could hear the impatience in her voice downstairs. She ran out of her room and leaned over the rail.

"I can't find my backpack!" she cried out.

"You mean this one?" Her mother pulled the bag from the floor beside her.

"Oh," she replied, her shoulders sagging as she walked down the stairs.

"Let's go to school, Marrah." Her mother said with a small smile on her face as they walked out the door.

8. Part A
The reason that Marrah missed the bus was that _____.

Ⓐ her mother didn't wake her up on time
Ⓑ she wasn't dressed yet
Ⓒ she couldn't find her backpack
Ⓓ she was still eating breakfast

Part B
Marrah looked under her sheets and pushed around mounds of clothes in her room, because _____.

Ⓐ she was looking for her backpack
Ⓑ she missed the bus
Ⓒ she couldn't decide what to wear to school
Ⓓ her mom told her to clean her room

Challenge Yourself!

- **Multiply Fractions**
- **Text Relationships**

https://www.lumoslearning.com/a/dc5-15

Day 5

See Page 7 for Signup details

Draw and Color

Use the below space for your drawing activity.

This Week's Online Activities

- **Reading Assignment**
- **Vocabulary Practice**
- **Write Your Summer Diary**

https://www.lumoslearning.com/a/slh5-6

See Page 7 for Signup details

Weekly Fun Summer Photo Contest

Take a picture of your summer fun activity and share it on Twitter or Instagram

Use the **#SummerLearning** mention

@LumosLearning on Twitter or

@lumos.learning on Instagram

Tag friends and increase your chances of winning the contest

Participate and stand a chance to WIN $50 Amazon gift card!

Week 4 Summer Practice

Multiply to Find Area (5.NF.B.4.B)

1. Dominique is covering the top of her desk with contact paper. The surface measures $\frac{7}{8}$ yard by $\frac{3}{4}$ yard. How much contact paper will she need to cover the surface of the desk top?

   Ⓐ $\frac{21}{32}$ yd²

   Ⓑ $\frac{13}{8}$ yd²

   Ⓒ $\frac{20}{24}$ yd²

   Ⓓ $1\frac{5}{8}$ yd²

2. Christopher is tiling his bathroom floor with tiles that are each 1 square foot. The floor measures $2\frac{1}{2}$ feet by $3\frac{3}{4}$ feet. How many tiles will he need to cover the floor?

   Ⓐ $6\frac{3}{8}$

   Ⓑ $6\frac{1}{4}$

   Ⓒ $9\frac{3}{8}$

   Ⓓ 8

3. Lin and Tyra are measuring the area of the piece of paper shown below. Lin multiplied the length times the width to find an answer. Tyra traced the paper onto 1-inch graph paper and counted the number of squares. How should their answers compare?

   (11 in. / 8 ½ in.)

   Ⓐ Lin's answer will be a mixed number, but Tyra's will be a whole number.
   Ⓑ Tyra's answer will be greater than Lin's answer.
   Ⓒ Lin's answer will be greater than Tyra's answer.
   Ⓓ They should end up with almost exactly the same answer.

4. **Use the picture below to find the area of the rectangle. Enter your answer in the box.**

$\frac{5}{6}$ cm

2 cm

Day 1

5. **What is a reference source?**

Ⓐ Sets of information that an author can base an article or story from such as almanacs, newspapers, and interviews
Ⓑ The actual text that an author uses to write an article or story
Ⓒ A set of information that is only valid in its primary form
Ⓓ A set of information that is only valid in its secondary form

6 **What does a 'prompt' mean with respect to "language?"**

Ⓐ A prompt details what the passage is about.
Ⓑ A prompt is a basic idea of what to write about.
Ⓒ A prompt forms the middle part of an essay.
Ⓓ A prompt is the conclusion of the passage.

Salmon

A fish that is a great favorite with people is salmon. It begins its life in a small pool up a river. Far from the sea, the fish lays its eggs in a pool in the river. When the baby fish are a few inches long, they begin to swim down the river. As they grow bigger, they make their way towards the sea.

They jump over rocks, often with their tails first. Suddenly, they find themselves in the sea. The fish live in the sea for three years. They swim far away from land. How do they find their way back? These fish have a wonderful sense of smell. They remember the scent of their journey easily
because the river flowed to the sea and carried them there. After three years, most salmon swim toward the pools.

As soon as they reach a pool, the females lay their eggs. They lay their eggs near the edge of the water and cover them with sand. Soon the eggs <u>hatch</u> , and the pool is full of small fish, getting ready for the long journey out to the sea.

As soon as they reach a pool, the females lay their eggs. They lay their eggs near the edge of the water and cover them with sand. Soon the eggs <u>hatch</u> and the pool is full of small fish, getting ready for the long journey out to the sea.

7. What is the meaning of the underlined word?

Ⓐ devise
Ⓑ produce
Ⓒ shade
Ⓓ emerge

We have been studying the <u>aftermath</u> of volcanos. Now I have to prepare an essay that includes this information.

8. What is the meaning of the underlined word?

Ⓐ cause
Ⓑ preparation
Ⓒ consequences
Ⓓ reason

Challenge Yourself!

- **Multiply to Find Area**
- **General Academic Vocabulary**

https://www.lumoslearning.com/a/dc5-16

Day 1

See Page 7 for Signup details

Day 2

1. If y is four times as much as z, which number completes this equation?

z * ___ = y

Ⓐ 4

Ⓑ 0.4

Ⓒ $\dfrac{1}{5}$

Ⓓ 40

2. In the equation a * b = c, if b is a fraction greater than 1, then c will be _____.

Ⓐ a mixed number
Ⓑ less than b
Ⓒ greater than a
Ⓓ equal to b ÷ 10

3. If d * e = f, and e is a fraction less than 1, then f will be _____.

Ⓐ greater than d
Ⓑ less than d
Ⓒ equal to e ÷ d
Ⓓ less than 1

4. Enter whether multiplying by a fraction >1 or <1 will give the correct answer. For this, enter <1 or <1 in the blanks given

$\dfrac{8}{9}$	×		<	$\dfrac{8}{9}$
	×	$1\dfrac{1}{5}$	<	$1\dfrac{1}{5}$
$\dfrac{5}{4}$	×		>	$\dfrac{5}{4}$

5. What is an index?

Ⓐ It is a sequential arrangement of names, places, and topics along with the page numbers that they are discussed on.
Ⓑ It is a list that helps in finding things pertaining to the topic faster.
Ⓒ Both A and B
Ⓓ None of the above

6. What is a glossary?

Ⓐ A list of unusual words
Ⓑ A list explaining or defining the difficult words and expressions used in the text
Ⓒ A list of where a word can be found in the book
Ⓓ Both B and C

Salmon

A fish that is a great favorite with people is salmon. It begins its life in a small pool up a river. Far from the sea, the fish lays its eggs in a pool in the river. When the baby fish are a few inches long, they begin to swim down the river. As they grow bigger, they make their way towards the sea.

They jump over rocks, often with their tails first. Suddenly, they find themselves in the sea. The fish live in the sea for three years. They swim far away from land. How do they find their way back? These fish have a wonderful sense of smell. They remember the scent of their journey easily because the river flowed to the sea and carried them there. After three years, most salmon swim toward the pools.

As soon as they reach a pool, the females lay their eggs. They lay their eggs near the edge of the water and cover them with sand. Soon the eggs hatch, and the pool is full of small fish, getting ready for the long journey out to the sea.

7. What genre would the writing above be classified as?

Ⓐ A nonfiction passage
Ⓑ Informative writing
Ⓒ Realistic fiction
Ⓓ Both A and B

We have been studying the aftermath of volcanoes. Now I have to prepare an essay that includes this information.

8. What type of text structure would best address this information?

Circle the correct answer choice.

Ⓐ cause and effect
Ⓑ problem and solution
Ⓒ chronological order
Ⓓ compare and contrast

Challenge Yourself!

- **Multiplication as Scaling**
- **Text Structure**

https://www.lumoslearning.com/a/dc5-17

Day 2

See Page 7 for Signup details

Day 3

1. **Which statement is true about the following equation?**
    $$6,827 \times \frac{2}{7} = ?$$

    Ⓐ The product will be less than 6,827.
    Ⓑ The product will be greater than 6,827.
    Ⓒ The product will be less than $\frac{2}{7}$.
    Ⓓ The product will be equal to $6,827 \div 7$.

2. **Which statement is true about the following equation?**
    $$27,093 \times \frac{5}{4} = ?$$

    Ⓐ The product will be equal to $27,093 \div 54$.
    Ⓑ The product will be less than $\frac{5}{4}$.
    Ⓒ The product will be less than 27,093.
    Ⓓ The product will be greater than 27,093.

3. **Estimate the product:**
    $$18,612 \times 1\frac{1}{7} = \underline{\hspace{3cm}}$$

    Ⓐ 15,000
    Ⓑ 21,000
    Ⓒ 38,000
    Ⓓ 2,500

4. **Which number completes the equation?**
    3,606 x ___ = 4,808
    Enter your answer in the box given below

Mary sat in front of Peter in the classroom. She had two long blonde braids in the back of her hair. Peter reached out and tugged on her braids. Mary turned around and swatted Peter with her notebook.

5. Identify the point of view used in the paragraph above.

Ⓐ first person
Ⓑ second person
Ⓒ third person
Ⓓ none of the above

It was a cool, crisp morning. Lucy threw her backpack over her shoulders, jumped on her bicycle, and pedaled down Pine Street. Her tires made soft crunching noises as she drove through piles of brown, yellow, and orange leaves.

6. Identify the point of view used in the paragraph above.

Ⓐ first person
Ⓑ second person
Ⓒ third person
Ⓓ none of the above

Mrs. Davis lived in a great big apartment on the top floor of her building. As I walked into her spacious, clean apartment, I noticed fine, leather furniture, and expensive works of art.

Mrs. Davis sat up in her large, king-size bed wearing a beautiful, silk robe and smiled at me. She looked like she felt better than she had the last time I visited.

7. Identify the point of view used in the paragraph above.

Ⓐ first person
Ⓑ second person
Ⓒ third person
Ⓓ none of the above

At the bakery, Vince, the baker, was getting the muffins ready for baking. He mixed up flour, sugar, milk, and blueberries. He poured the mixture into a muffin pan and placed it into the oven. Then, he heard one of his employees call him from the front of the store. "A lady wants six blueberry muffins!" "Ok," Vince called back, "I'll have them ready in ten minutes!"

8. Identify the point of view of the paragraph above.

- Ⓐ first person
- Ⓑ second person
- Ⓒ third person
- Ⓓ none of the above

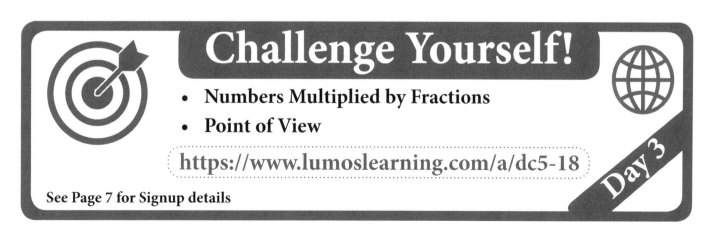

Challenge Yourself!

- **Numbers Multiplied by Fractions**
- **Point of View**

https://www.lumoslearning.com/a/dc5-18

See Page 7 for Signup details

Day 3

Day 4

1. Chef Chris is using $\frac{3}{4}$ lb. of chicken per person at a luncheon. If there are 17 people at the luncheon, how many pounds of chicken will he use?

   Ⓐ $12\frac{3}{4}$

   Ⓑ $\frac{51}{68}$

   Ⓒ $\frac{48}{4}$

   Ⓓ $17\frac{3}{4}$

2. A team of runners ran a relay race $\frac{9}{10}$ of a mile long. If Carl ran $\frac{3}{5}$ of the race, how far did his teammates run?

   Ⓐ $\frac{9}{25}$ mile

   Ⓑ $\frac{27}{50}$ mile

   Ⓒ $\frac{1}{10}$ mile

   Ⓓ $\frac{2}{5}$ mile

3. There are $1\frac{4}{5}$ lbs. of jelly beans in each bag. If Mrs. Lancer buys 3 bags of jelly beans for her class, how many pounds of jelly beans will she have in all?

   Ⓐ $3\frac{12}{15}$

   Ⓑ $5\frac{2}{5}$

   Ⓒ $3\frac{4}{15}$

   Ⓓ $5\frac{4}{5}$

4. Kendra ran 6 miles. Her friend Riley ran $\frac{2}{3}$ as far as Kendra. How far did Riley run? Simplify the answer and enter it in the box.

Day 4

What is this life if, full of care,
We have no time to stand and stare?

No time to stand beneath the boughs
And stare as long as sheep or cows.

No time to see, when woods we pass,
Where squirrels hide their nuts in grass

No time to see, in broad daylight,
Streams full of stars, like skies at night.

No time to turn at Beauty's glance,
And watch her feet, how they can dance.

No time to wait till her mouth can
Enrich that smile her eyes began.

A poor life if, full of care,
We have no time to stand and stare.
- W. H. Davies

5. If you had to research the poet above, where would you look for information?

Ⓐ in the library
Ⓑ on the Internet
Ⓒ in a book about different poets
Ⓓ all of the above

I went for a run this morning. Although I usually run in the evening, I decided to go in the morning because of the weather. It has been so hot this summer, so hot in fact, that I cannot run in the evening. Therefore, until we have cooler weather, I will continue to enjoy a morning run.

6. Where might you find the passage above?

Ⓐ You might find it in a newspaper.
Ⓑ You might find it on the Internet.
Ⓒ You might find it in a journal or diary.
Ⓓ You might find it in a book report.

7. Read each of the statement and match it with the place in which you can locate it in a text book

	Table of Contents	glossary	Index	copyright page
where would you look to locate a chapter on the Civil War	◯	◯	◯	◯
where would you look to locate the definition of a key word	◯	◯	◯	◯
where would you look to locate the alphabetical list of important topics	◯	◯	◯	◯
where would you look to locate when the book was published	◯	◯	◯	◯

8. In a textbook, where can additional information such as additional charts and graphs be found? Circle the correct answer choice.

Ⓐ Appendix
Ⓑ Index
Ⓒ Table of Contents
Ⓓ Glossary

Challenge Yourself!

- **Real World Problems with Fractions**
- **Locating Answers**

https://www.lumoslearning.com/a/dc5-19

Day 4

See Page 7 for Signup details

Day 5

1. Divide: $2 \div \dfrac{1}{3} =$

- Ⓐ 3
- Ⓑ 2
- Ⓒ 1
- Ⓓ 6

2. In order to divide by a fraction you must first:

- Ⓐ find its reciprocal
- Ⓑ match its denominator
- Ⓒ find its factors
- Ⓓ multiply by the numerator

3. Divide: $3 \div \dfrac{2}{3} =$

- Ⓐ $4 \dfrac{2}{3}$
- Ⓑ $3 \dfrac{2}{3}$
- Ⓒ 4
- Ⓓ $4 \dfrac{1}{2}$

4. Read each equation below and mark whether the equation is true or false.

	True	False
$6 \div \dfrac{1}{3} > 16$	○	○
$\dfrac{1}{4} \div 3 = \dfrac{3}{12}$	○	○
$12 \div \dfrac{1}{6} < 80$	○	○
$\dfrac{1}{5} \div 2 > 9$	○	○

The Orange

Even though no one knows exactly where oranges come from, Southeast Asia is believed to be their first home. They are grown today in most of the warmer parts of the world. The ancient Greeks and Romans knew about oranges. It is possible that oranges were carried from India to Western Asia and then to Europe.

The Spaniards took the sour oranges to the West Indies and from there to Florida, in America. Today, oranges are the most important fresh fruit in international trade. There are three different kinds of oranges: the sweet or common orange, the mandarin orange, and the sour or bitter orange.

One type of sweet orange is called the blood orange. It has a pulp with a deep red color. This type of orange is grown mostly in the Mediterranean region. Mandarin oranges are mainly found in Florida. Sour oranges are grown almost everywhere, with Spain having the greatest number used for trade. These sour oranges are generally used to make marmalade.

However, they can be put to many other interesting uses, from making medicine to creating perfumes. Oranges have many medicinal values. Oranges are the fruit with the greatest concentration of vitamin C. The skin of the orange helps to keep the fruit inside from becoming damaged and to remain clean. The thick, oily, and bitter skin does not allow any insects to get into an orange. Many kinds of useful oils can be extracted from the thick skin. Oranges are healthy and delicious.

5. Which paragraph discusses the types of oranges?

Ⓐ paragraph one
Ⓑ paragraph two
Ⓒ paragraph three
Ⓓ paragraph four

6. Which paragraph discusses the health value of oranges?

Ⓐ paragraph one
Ⓑ paragraph two
Ⓒ paragraph three
Ⓓ paragraph four

Oranges

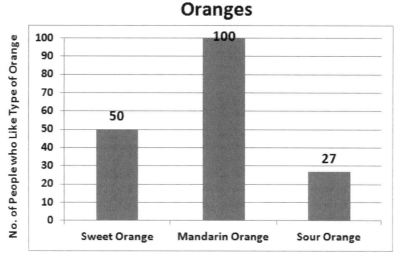

Types of Oranges

7. According the graph, which type of orange is the most popular?

Ⓐ Sweet Orange
Ⓑ Mandarin Orange
Ⓒ Sour Orange

8. Select the phrase that best completes the sentence and Circle the correct answer choice

Evidence to support details can be found _____.

Ⓐ in the text and title only
Ⓑ in the text only
Ⓒ in the text, illustrations, graphs, and headings
Ⓓ in the conclusion

Challenge Yourself!

- **Dividing Fractions**
- **Using Evidence to Support Claims**

https://www.lumoslearning.com/a/dc5-20

Day 5

See Page 7 for Signup details

6 Tips to Better Your Basketball Skills

1.   Dribble With Your Weak Hand

One of the most important aspects of the game of basketball is dribbling, which is why it is important to be a skilled dribbler with both hands. It's easy to dribble with your dominant hand because you feel more in control of the ball; however, sometimes, it's necessary to dribble with your opposite hand. A skilled ball handler practices dribbling with their weak hand until, eventually, it feels just as natural. You can practice this during drills, and even on your own, all you need is a basketball and something to dribble on. Try walking around the block while dribbling with your nondominant hand or switch which hand you usually use during your team's practices.

2.   Box Out

Once a shot goes up, it's important to find your nearest opponent and box out. Boxing out means using your body to get in between the basket and a person on the opposing team to try and get the rebound. If you don't box out, it's easy for the other team to catch the rebound and put up another shot or gain possession of the ball. The best technique for boxing out is, once someone shoots, to find the nearest person from the other team and use your behind to move them away from the basket. You're going to want to get low and use your body, rather than your hands, to move them because using your hands is against the rules and the referee will call a foul on you.

3.   Remember B.E.E.F. when shooting foul shots

It sounds silly, but B.E.E.F. is proven to help you make foul shots. It stands for Bend, Elbow, Eyes, Follow through. When you're on the line to shoot a foul shot, you're first going to want to bend your knees. A foul shot needs to be shot using power from your whole body, and bending your knees helps you use your legs in your shot. Next is elbow- make sure that your shooting arm is bent in front of you, and your elbow lines up with the basket. Once your elbow is towards the basket, focus your eyes just over the rim. This helps you visualize where the ball needs to go, which makes it easier to hit your target. Once you're ready to shoot, you're going to want to follow through with your shot. The foul shot uses muscles from your whole body, not just your arms, and if you shot correctly, you should end your shot on your toes with your shooting arm in the air. This helps you use all of the power in your body to shoot the ball. It might take a little bit of practice, but if you follow B.E.E.F. your foul shots will improve in no time.

4.   Pass with a Purpose

Passing is the quickest way to get the ball from one place to another on the court. There are a couple of different types of passes (bounce pass, chest pass, overhead pass), but regardless of the type of pass, all passes should be done with a purpose. If you pass the ball just to get rid of it, it's likely to get stolen by the other team, however, if you confidently pass to a teammate, the chance of it getting stolen is much lower. You're also going to want to pass with power- a pass without strength behind it is not the kind of pass you want to make. A strong pass gets to your teammate faster and is less likely to be intercepted by the other team. To practice making strong passes, try passing with a friend in your spare time, or, if another person isn't around, practice your passes against a wall outside (make sure you get permission first!!).

5.   Practice Off the Court

The best part about basketball is that it's very easy to practice your skills outside of your team's practice- all you need is a ball and something to bounce it on! You can practice dribbling, passing, even shooting, without a court in sight. Dribble the ball in your driveway or on the sidewalk, pass against a wall or with a friend, practice your shooting form- all of these can be done with only a ball and your passion for the game. As basketball legends, all say, "Don't practice until you get it right. Practice until you can't get it wrong".

6.   Conditioning Matters

One of the most forgotten skills of basketball is conditioning. Everyone always focuses on dribbling, shooting, and passing, but never the endurance and stamina needed for basketball. Basketball is a fast-paced sport- everyone is constantly sprinting around the court and running to make plays. The only time anyone ever stops hustling is during timeouts! The fast-paced nature of the game makes it important to practice conditioning to keep up with the speed of the game. Go for runs around your neighborhood or practice sprinting around the court when you practice. This helps you build your endurance and makes it easier for you to play the game at your top speed.

This Week's Online Activities

- **Reading Assignment**
- **Vocabulary Practice**
- **Write Your Summer Diary**

https://www.lumoslearning.com/a/slh5-6

See Page 7 for Signup details

Weekly Fun Summer Photo Contest

Take a picture of your summer fun activity and share it on Twitter or Instagram

Use the **#SummerLearning** mention

@LumosLearning on Twitter or

@lumos.learning on Instagram

Tag friends and increase your chances of winning the contest

Participate and stand a chance to WIN $50 Amazon gift card!

Dividing by Unit Fractions (5.NF.B.7.B)

Day 1

1. Which best explains why $6 \div \dfrac{1}{4} = 24$?

   Ⓐ $24 \div \dfrac{1}{4} = 6$

   Ⓑ $24 \times \dfrac{1}{4} = 6$

   Ⓒ $24 \div 6 = \dfrac{1}{4}$

   Ⓓ $24 = \dfrac{1}{4} \times 6$

2. Which model best represents the following equation?

   $$4 \div \dfrac{1}{3} = 12$$

   Ⓐ

   Ⓑ

   Ⓒ

   Ⓓ

3. **Which equation matches this model?**

(A) $24 \div \dfrac{1}{8} = 3$

(B) $24 \div \dfrac{1}{3} = 8$

(C) $8 \div \dfrac{1}{3} = 24$

(D) $3 \div \dfrac{1}{8} = 24$

4. **Read each statement below and indicate whether it is true or false.**

Statements	True	False
$\dfrac{1}{12} \div 4 > 40$	◯	◯
$\dfrac{1}{4} \div 7 = \dfrac{1}{14}$	◯	◯
$\dfrac{1}{3} \div 33 < 5$	◯	◯
$\dfrac{1}{8} \div 4 < \dfrac{1}{2}$	◯	◯

Integrating Information (RI.5.9)

Day 1

5. **In which situation would you possibly need to read multiple texts?**

(A) to locate an answer to a question
(B) to write or speak about a topic knowledgeably
(C) to fully understand a historical or scientific concept
(D) all of the above

6. If you are studying World War II, you might _____.

Fill in the blank after choosing the correct option from among the 4 options given below

Ⓐ read a chapter from your social studies textbook about World War II
Ⓑ look at a book of photographs from the war
Ⓒ read a magazine article written by someone who fought in the war
Ⓓ all of the above

SAR Dogs

Search-and-rescue (SAR) dogs are special dogs with an acute sense of smell that are called in when a person is lost or trapped. SAR dogs search in remote areas and in places struck by natural disasters such as earthquakes, tornadoes, and hurricanes. SAR dogs are very effective and can often locate people when many volunteers can't.

Dogs make great searchers because of their powerful sense of smell. SAR dogs are trained to use their incredible sense of smell to search for people.

In 2010, SAR dogs from the United States found people trapped in the rubble after a devastating earthquake in Haiti. In 2012, SAR dogs helped locate people who were trapped in their homes after Hurricane Sandy hit the East Coast. These are only a few instances when SAR dogs have helped people.

7. Part A
What is the girls' attitude toward SAR dogs?

Ⓐ They are scared of them.
Ⓑ They are angry at them.
Ⓒ They are thankful for them.
Ⓓ They make them sad.

Part B
How does information from "SAR Dogs" add to your understanding of the story "Lost in the Woods?"

Ⓐ It explains that the dogs' sense of smell helps them find people.
Ⓑ It helps the reader to understand the setting of the story.
Ⓒ It helps the reader to get to know the characters better.
Ⓓ It informs the reader about natural disasters of the past.

8. From which type of point of view is SAR Dogs told?

Ⓐ first person
Ⓑ objective
Ⓒ subjective
Ⓓ none of the above

 **Challenge Yourself!**

- **Dividing by Unit Fractions**
- **Integrating Information**

https://www.lumoslearning.com/a/dc5-21

Day 1

See Page 7 for Signup details

1. Darren has a 3 cup bag of snack mix. Each serving is $\frac{1}{4}$ cup. Which model will help him determine how many $\frac{1}{4}$ cup servings are in the whole bag of snack mix?

Ⓐ

Ⓑ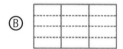

Ⓒ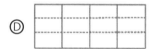

Ⓓ

2. Which situation could be represented by the following model?

Ⓐ The number of $\frac{1}{8}$ lb. servings of cheese in 4 lbs. of cheese

Ⓑ Four friends share 8 lbs. of cheese

Ⓒ 4 lbs. of cheese divided into 8 equal servings

Ⓓ The amount of cheese needed for 8 people to each have $\frac{1}{4}$ lb.

3. A team of 3 runners competes in a $\frac{1}{4}$ mile relay race. If each person runs an equal portion of the race, how far does each person run?

Ⓐ $\frac{3}{7}$ mile

Ⓑ $\frac{3}{12}$ mile

Ⓒ $\frac{3}{4}$ mile

Ⓓ $\frac{1}{12}$ mile

4. Mrs. Klein has a small rectangular area in her back yard to use for composting. If the width of the rectangular area is $1\frac{1}{7}$ yards and the compost area must be less than 6 square yards, what is the maximum length of the garden?
Enter your answer in the box below.

Prepositional Phrases (L.5.1.A)

Day 2

5. Prepositions are _____ .

Ⓐ words that introduce or connect
Ⓑ words that confuse
Ⓒ words that show action
Ⓓ words that end a sentence

We met at the loud concert.

6. Identify the preposition in the above sentence.

Ⓐ we
Ⓑ met
Ⓒ at
Ⓓ concert

7. The object of a preposition is _____.

    Ⓐ the actual preposition
    Ⓑ the noun or pronoun that follows the preposition
    Ⓒ a word that identifies
    Ⓓ a word that shows direction

8. Select the preposition that best completes the sentence by circling it.

Tomorrow will be the third day we have lived ____ the new house.

    Ⓐ in
    Ⓑ on
    Ⓒ at
    Ⓓ with

Challenge Yourself!

- **Real World Problems Dividing Fractions**
- **Prepositional Phrases**

https://www.lumoslearning.com/a/dc5-22

Day 2

See Page 7 for Signup details

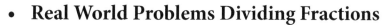

Day 3

1. Complete the following.
   1 inch equals the same length as _____ centimeters.

   Ⓐ 0.6
   Ⓑ 2.54
   Ⓒ 10
   Ⓓ 2.0

2. Complete the following.
   10 cm = 1 ___

   Ⓐ km
   Ⓑ dm
   Ⓒ mm
   Ⓓ m

3. Keith has 7 yards of string. How many inches of string does he have?

   Ⓐ 112 inches
   Ⓑ 224 inches
   Ⓒ 84 inches
   Ⓓ 252 inches

4. A meter is 100 centimeters. If a track is 500 meters long. How long is the track in centimeters? Enter your answer in the box given below.

Mrs. Smith <u>teach</u> us math this year.

5. What is the correct way to write the underlined verb?

Ⓐ teaches
Ⓑ taught
Ⓒ teaching
Ⓓ teached

6. In which sentence is the verb *have* used correctly?

Ⓐ Emily have a wonderful dinner last night.
Ⓑ I have lemon cake for dessert tomorrow.
Ⓒ She have chocolate chip cookies today.
Ⓓ I have brownies for a snack.

7. In which of the following sentences can the verb <u>climbing</u> be used correctly?

Ⓐ I _____ the mountain last year.
Ⓑ My mother and I _____ three flights of stairs.
Ⓒ Maggie went rock _____ at the gym yesterday.
Ⓓ Yesterday, my sister said I could _____ to the top of the highest hill.

8. Fruits <u>beginning</u> to appear on the orange trees when they are three years old.
What is the correct way to write the underlined verb?
Enter your answer in the box given below.

Challenge Yourself!

- **Converting Units of Measure**
- **Verbs**

https://www.lumoslearning.com/a/dc5-23

Day 3

See Page 7 for Signup details

Day 4

1. **A 5th grade science class is raising mealworms. The students measured the mealworms and recorded the lengths on this line plot.**

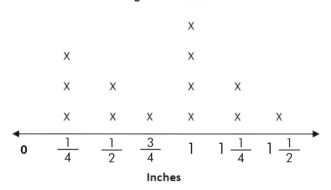

According to this line plot, what was the length of the longest mealworm?

Ⓐ $1\frac{1}{2}$ inches

Ⓑ $\frac{3}{4}$ inch

Ⓒ $\frac{1}{4}$ inch

Ⓓ 1 inch

2. **A 5th grade science class is raising mealworms. The students measured the mealworms and recorded the lengths on this line plot.**

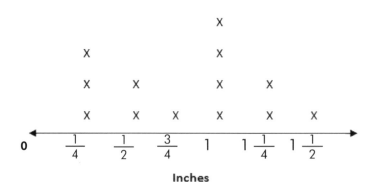

According to this line plot, what was the length of the shortest mealworm?

Ⓐ $\frac{1}{4}$ inch

Ⓑ $\frac{3}{4}$ inch

Ⓒ $1\frac{1}{4}$ inch

Ⓓ 0

3. A 5th grade science class is raising mealworms. The students measured the mealworms and recorded the lengths on this line plot.

Length of Mealworms

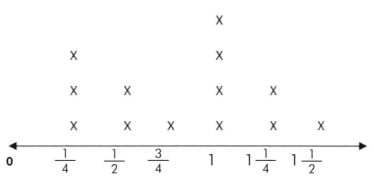

Inches

According to this line plot, what was the most common length for mealworms?

Ⓐ $1\frac{1}{2}$ inches

Ⓑ $\frac{3}{4}$ inch

Ⓒ $\frac{1}{4}$ inch

Ⓓ 1 inch

4. The line plot below shows the length in fractions of an inch of several pieces of tile all having the same width. If the pieces were lined up length to length, how long would the line of tiles be? Circle the correct answer.

Ⓐ $3\frac{1}{4}$

Ⓑ $3\frac{5}{8}$

Ⓒ $1\frac{4}{8}$

Ⓓ $4\frac{5}{8}$

Day 4

The video game my sister ____ _____ broke, and it is all her fault.

5. Select the correct form of the verb to complete the above sentence.

    Ⓐ are playing
    Ⓑ were playing
    Ⓒ was playing
    Ⓓ will play

_____ are the reason we are late today.

6. Select the correct subject to complete the above sentence.

    Ⓐ She
    Ⓑ They
    Ⓒ He
    Ⓓ Her

7. Although she has been able to practice, she can never perfect the backflip.

Identify the verb phrase in the below sentence.
Enter your answer in the box given below

8. As salmon grow bigger, they make their way towards the sea. They jump over rocks, often with their tails first. Suddenly, they find themselves in the sea.

What tense are the verbs in this paragraph?
Enter your answer in the box given below

Challenge Yourself!

- **Representing and Interpreting Data**
- **Subject-Verb Agreement**

https://www.lumoslearning.com/a/dc5-24

Day 4

See Page 7 for Signup details

Day 5

1. Which type of unit might be used to record the volume of a rectangular prism?

    Ⓐ inches
    Ⓑ square inches
    Ⓒ ounces
    Ⓓ cubic inches

2. Maeve needed to pack a crate that measured 4 ft. by 2 ft. by 3 ft. with 1 foot cubes. How many 1 foot cubes can she fit in the crate?

    Ⓐ 12 cubes
    Ⓑ 48 cubes
    Ⓒ 24 cubes
    Ⓓ 9 cubes

3   The volume of an object is the amount of _____.

    Ⓐ space it occupies
    Ⓑ dimensions it has
    Ⓒ layers you can put in it
    Ⓓ weight it can hold

4. Oscar wants to determine the volume of the chest, shown in the picture, in cubic inches. Complete the sentence below describing the dimensions of the unit cube.

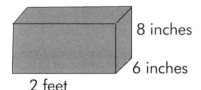

8 inches

6 inches

2 feet

Unit cube length	
Unit cube width	
Unit cube height	

5. **These words are used to modify and describe nouns and pronouns.**

Ⓐ Adjectives
Ⓑ Adverbs
Ⓒ Nouns
Ⓓ Verbs

6. **These words are used to modify or describe verbs or adverbs.**

Ⓐ Adjectives
Ⓑ Adverbs
Ⓒ Nouns
Ⓓ Verbs

She makes the most _____ chocolate chip cookies. They are so good that the most _____ bakery in the nation wants her recipe.

7. **Select the answer that has the correct adjectives in the correct order to complete the sentence.**

Ⓐ delicious, famous
Ⓑ famous, delicious
Ⓒ deliciouser, famouser
Ⓓ delicious, all famous

Robin works <u>here.</u>

8. **What part of speech is the underlined word in the above sentence? Enter your answer in the box given below**

Challenge Yourself!

• **Volume**

• **Adjectives and Adverbs**

https://www.lumoslearning.com/a/dc5-25

Day 5

See Page 7 for Signup details

Maze Game

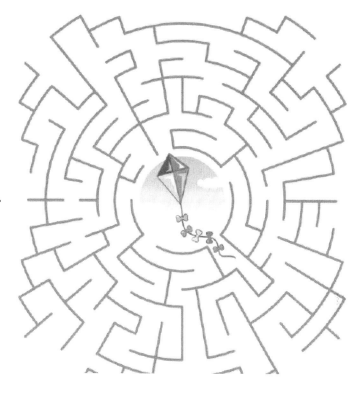

Help the beautiful kite fly out of the maze.

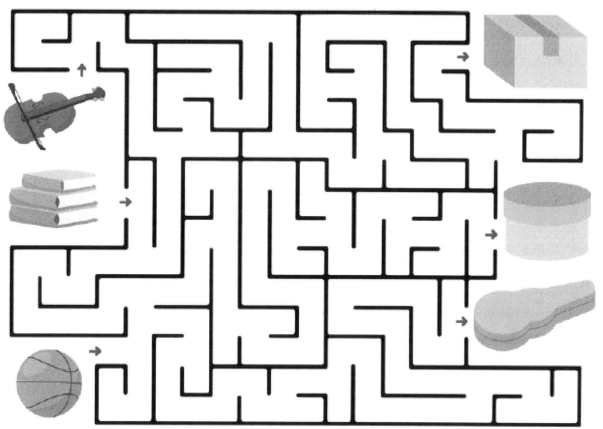

This Week's Online Activities

- **Reading Assignment**
- **Vocabulary Practice**
- **Write Your Summer Diary**

https://www.lumoslearning.com/a/slh5-6

See Page 7 for Signup details

Weekly Fun Summer Photo Contest

Take a picture of your summer fun activity and share it on Twitter or Instagram

Use the **#SummerLearning** mention

@LumosLearning on Twitter or

@lumos.learning on Instagram

Tag friends and increase your chances of winning the contest

Participate and stand a chance to WIN $50 Amazon gift card!

1. Stan covers the bottom of a box with 8 centimeter cubes, leaving no gaps. He is able to build 4 layers of cubes to fill the box completely. What is the volume of the box?

   Ⓐ 32 centimeters
   Ⓑ The square of 32 cm
   Ⓒ 32 cm^2
   Ⓓ 32 cubic centimeters

2. Which of these is an accurate way to measure the volume of a rectangular prism?

   Ⓐ Fill it with water and then weigh the water.
   Ⓑ Trace each face of the prism on centimeter grid paper, and then count the number of squares it comprises.
   Ⓒ Measure the length and the width, and then multiply the two values.
   Ⓓ Pack it with unit cubes, leaving no gaps or overlaps, and count the number of unit cubes.

3. Which of these could possibly be the volume of a cereal box?

   Ⓐ 360 in^3
   Ⓑ 520 sq cm
   Ⓒ 400 cubic feet
   Ⓓ 385 dm^2

4. Select the picture that has a volume of 12 cubic units.
   Key: ☐ represents one cubic unit

Ⓐ

Ⓑ

Ⓒ

Ⓓ

Danielle wants _____ pizza _____ pasta for lunch, because she doesn't like Italian food.

5. Which set of conjunctions correctly completes the sentence?

Ⓐ either, or
Ⓑ neither, and
Ⓒ neither, nor
Ⓓ either, and

I can't decide _____ I should take Spanish class next year _____ German class.

6. Which set of conjunctions correctly completes the sentence?

Ⓐ either, or
Ⓑ whether, or
Ⓒ neither, nor
Ⓓ whether, nor

_____ my mom _____ my dad can take me to the library.

7. Which set of conjunctions correctly completes the sentence?

Ⓐ Whether, or
Ⓑ Neither, nor
Ⓒ Either, nor
Ⓓ Whether, nor

8. Which of the following are pairs of correlative conjunctions? Circle the correct answer choice

Ⓐ either, or
Ⓑ neither, nor
Ⓒ whether, or
Ⓓ all of the above

Challenge Yourself!

- **Cubic Units**
- **Correlative Conjunctions**

https://www.lumoslearning.com/a/dc5-26

Day 1

See Page 7 for Signup details

Counting Cubic Units (5.MD.C.4)

1. What is the volume of the figure?

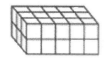

    Ⓐ 60 cubic units
    Ⓑ 15 cubic units
    Ⓒ 30 cubic units
    Ⓓ 31 cubic units

2. What is the volume of the figure?

    Ⓐ 30 units^3
    Ⓑ 27 units^3
    Ⓒ 31 units^3
    Ⓓ 36 units^3

3. Which of these has a volume of 24 cubic units?

Ⓐ

Ⓑ

Ⓒ

Ⓓ

4. Garrett must build a building that has a volume of 11 cubic meters. Look at the buildings below and indicate which are possible designs for his building.
Volume of one cube is one cubic meter.

	Yes	No
	○	○
	○	○
	○	○
	○	○

Day 2

5. Which sentence is written correctly?

Ⓐ My Cat, Katie, is black and white.
Ⓑ My cat, Katie, is black and white.
Ⓒ my Cat, Katie, is black and white.
Ⓓ My cat, katie, is black and white.

6. Select the sentence that uses capital letters correctly.

Ⓐ Nana has two Dogs, named Hank and Sugar, who love the Back Porch.
Ⓑ Nana has two Dogs, named Hank and Sugar, who love the back porch.
Ⓒ Nana has two dogs, named Hank and Sugar, who love the back porch.
Ⓓ nana has two dogs, named Hank and Sugar, who love the back porch.

7. Select the sentence that uses capital letters correctly.

Ⓐ "You just missed the bus!" Marrah's mother yelled. "Why can't you ever be on time?"
Ⓑ "You just missed the bus!" Marrah's Mother yelled. "Why can't you ever be on time?"
Ⓒ "you just missed the bus!" Marrah's mother yelled. "why can't you ever be on time?"
Ⓓ "You just missed the bus!" marrah's Mother yelled. "Why can't you ever be on time?"

8. Select the sentence that uses capital letters correctly.
Circle the correct answer choice

Ⓐ "Let's go, Marrah!" Her Mother called from downstairs. "You don't want to be late to school too!"
Ⓑ "Let's go, Marrah!" Her mother called from downstairs. "you don't want to be late to school too!"
Ⓒ "Let's go, Marrah!" Her mother called from downstairs. "You don't want to be late to school too!"
Ⓓ "Let's go, marrah!" Her Mother called from downstairs. "You don't want to be late to school too!"

Challenge Yourself!

- **Counting Cubic Units**
- **Capitalization**

https://www.lumoslearning.com/a/dc5-27

Day 2

See Page 7 for Signup details

1. What is the volume of the figure?

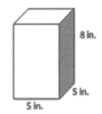

Ⓐ 33 in³

Ⓑ 18 in³

Ⓒ 80 in³

Ⓓ 200 in³

2. What is the volume of the figure?

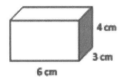

Ⓐ   **13 cm³**

Ⓑ   **22 cm³**

Ⓒ   **72 cm³**

Ⓓ   **700 cm³**

3. The figure has a volume of 66 ft³. What is the height of the figure?

Ⓐ   **11 ft**

Ⓑ   **61 ft**

Ⓒ   **13 ft**

Ⓓ   **33 ft**

4.   Piko filled a box with 4 layers of cubes that measured one foot on each side. If the bottom of the box fit 6 cubes, What is the volume of the box? Enter the answer in the box.

Day 3

5. Which sentence is written correctly?

Ⓐ Will your mom take us to school, or do we have to take the bus!
Ⓑ Will your Mom, take us to school, or do we have to take the bus.
Ⓒ Will your Mom, take us to school, or do we have to take the bus?
Ⓓ Will your Mom take us to school, or do we have to take the bus.

6. Which sentence has the correct punctuation?

Ⓐ After I scraped the gum off my shoes I went into the house!
Ⓑ After I scraped the gum off my shoes, I went into the house.
Ⓒ After I scraped the gum off my shoes I went into the house?
Ⓓ After, I scraped the gum off my shoes I went into the house.

7. Which sentence has the correct punctuation?

Ⓐ I have already seen the movie you want to see.
Ⓑ I have already seen, the movie you want to see!
Ⓒ I have already seen, the movie you want, to see.
Ⓓ I have, already seen the movie you want to see.

8. Which sentence has the correct punctuation?
Circle the correct answer choice

Ⓐ The boss entered the room and the workers became silent.
Ⓑ The boss, entered the room, and the workers became silent?
Ⓒ The boss entered the room, and the workers, became silent.
Ⓓ The boss entered the room, and the workers became silent.

Challenge Yourself!

- **Multiply to Find Volume**
- **Punctuation**

https://www.lumoslearning.com/a/dc5-28

Day 3

See Page 7 for Signup details

Day 4

1. Michael packed a box full of 1 ft cubes. The box held 54 cubes. Which of these could be the box Michael packed?

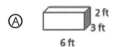

(A) 2 ft, 3 ft, 6 ft

(B) 9 ft, 2 ft, 3 ft

(C) 4 ft, 4 ft, 4 ft

(D) 2 ft, 1 ft, 18 ft

2. A container is shaped like a rectangular prism. The area of its base is 30 in². If the container is 5 inches tall, how many 1 inch cubes can it hold?

Ⓐ 150
Ⓑ 35
Ⓒ 4500
Ⓓ 95

3. A rectangular prism has a volume of 300 cm³. If the area of its base is 25 cm² how tall is the prism?

Ⓐ 325 cm
Ⓑ 7500 cm
Ⓒ 12 cm
Ⓓ 275 cm

4   A building has a volume of 1520 ft3 . The area of the base of the building is 95 ft².
Circle the volume of the box .

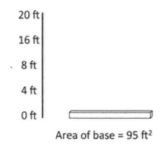

Area of base = 95 ft²

Ⓐ 20ft
Ⓑ 16ft
Ⓒ 8ft
Ⓓ 4ft

Commas in Introductory Phrases (L.5.2.B)

Day 4

An introductory phrase comes at the _____ of a sentence.

5. Which word correctly completes the sentence above?

Ⓐ   beginning
Ⓑ   middle
Ⓒ   end
Ⓓ   none of the above

6. Which sentence uses a comma in the correct place?

Ⓐ   After, the class returned from the playground they took a math test.
Ⓑ   After the class, returned from the playground they took a math test.
Ⓒ   After the class returned, from the playground they took a math test.
Ⓓ   After the class returned from the playground, they took a math test.

7. Which sentence uses a comma in the correct place?

Ⓐ If you, always eat breakfast you will be more successful in school.
Ⓑ If you always eat breakfast, you will be more successful in school.
Ⓒ If you always eat breakfast you will be more successful, in school.
Ⓓ If, you always eat breakfast you will be more successful in school.

8. Which sentence uses a comma in the correct place?

Ⓐ Until, the whole class gets quiet we will not start watching the video.
Ⓑ Until the whole class, gets quiet we will not start watching the video.
Ⓒ Until the whole class gets quiet, we will not start watching the video.
Ⓓ Until the whole class gets quiet we will not start, watching the video.

Challenge Yourself!

- **Real World Problems with Volume**
- **Commas in Introductory Phrases**

https://www.lumoslearning.com/a/dc5-29

Day 4

See Page 7 for Signup details

Day 5

1. A refrigerator has a 3 foot by 2 foot base. The refrigerator portion is 4 feet high and the freezer is 2 feet high. What is the total volume?

   Ⓐ 36 ft³
   Ⓑ 26 ft³
   Ⓒ 11 ft³
   Ⓓ 16 ft³

2. Matthew has two identical coolers. Each one measures 30 inches long, 10 inches wide, and 15 inches high. What is the total volume of the two coolers?

   Ⓐ 4,500 in³
   Ⓑ 9,000 in³
   Ⓒ 110 in³
   Ⓓ 3,025 in³

3. Ingrid is packing 1 foot square boxes into shipping crates. She has two shipping crates, shown below. How many boxes can she pack in them all together?

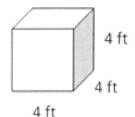 

4 ft
4 ft
4 ft

2 ft
1 ft
18 ft

   Ⓐ 64
   Ⓑ 33
   Ⓒ 82
   Ⓓ 100

4. A three-section warehouse holds a total of 24,766 ft cube of volume. The first section has a storage area of 436 ft square and a height of 19 ft. The second section has a height of 15 ft. and a depth of 26 ft. The volume of the first two sections is 17,254 ft cube. Based on this information, complete the table below.

Volume of first section in cubic feet	
Length of the second section in feet	
Volume of the third section in cubic feet	

Using Commas (L.5.2.C)

Day 5

5. Which sentence uses a comma in the correct place?

Ⓐ Sammy, may I go with you to the mall?
Ⓑ Sammy may I go, with you to the mall?
Ⓒ Sammy may I go with you, to the mall?
Ⓓ Sammy may I, go with you to the mall?

6. Which sentence uses commas correctly?

Ⓐ If I could play the guitar, like you Wally I would join a band.
Ⓑ If I could play the guitar like you, Wally I would join a band.
Ⓒ If I could play the guitar like you, Wally, I would join a band.
Ⓓ If I could play the guitar like you Wally, I would join a band.

7. Which sentence uses a comma in the correct place?
Circle the correct answer

Ⓐ Yes, I can help you edit your English essay.
Ⓑ Yes I can help you, edit your English essay.
Ⓒ Yes I can help, you edit your English essay.
Ⓓ Yes I can help you edit your English, essay.

8. Which sentence uses a comma in the correct place?
Circle the correct answer

(A) Beau can I come over, and play video games with you?
(B) Beau, can I come over and play video games with you?
(C) Beau, can I come over, and play video games with you?
(D) Beau can I come over and play video games, with you?

Challenge Yourself!

- **Adding Volumes**
- **Using Commas**

https://www.lumoslearning.com/a/dc5-30

Day 5

See Page 7 for Signup details

This Week's Online Activities

- **Reading Assignment**
- **Vocabulary Practice**
- **Write Your Summer Diary**

https://www.lumoslearning.com/a/slh5-6

See Page 7 for Signup details

Weekly Fun Summer Photo Contest

Take a picture of your summer fun activity and share it on Twitter or Instagram

Use the **#SummerLearning** mention

@LumosLearning on Twitter or

@lumos.learning on Instagram

Tag friends and increase your chances of winning the contest

Participate and stand a chance to WIN $50 Amazon gift card!

1. Assume Point D was added to the grid so that Shape ABCD was a rectangle. Which of these could be the ordered pair for Point D?

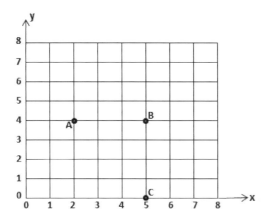

Ⓐ (0, 0)
Ⓑ (0, 2)
Ⓒ (2, 0)
Ⓓ (2, 2)

2. Assume Segments AB and BC were drawn. Compare the lengths of the two segments.

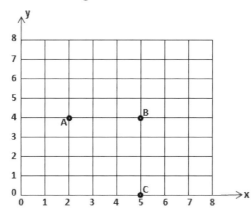

Ⓐ Segment AB is longer than Segment BC.
Ⓑ Segment BC is longer than Segment AB.
Ⓒ Segments AB and BC have the same length.
Ⓓ It cannot be determined from this information.

3.

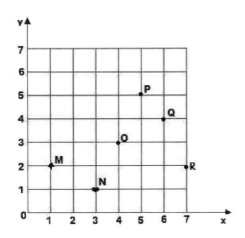

Where is Point R located?

Ⓐ (2, 7)
Ⓑ (7, 2)
Ⓒ (6, 4)
Ⓓ (4, 6)

4. Circle the letter that represents the x- axis.

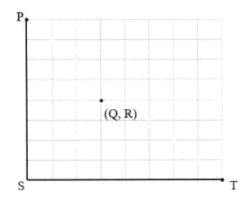

Ⓐ P
Ⓑ S
Ⓒ T

Writing Titles (L.5.2.D)

My favorite Shel Silverstein poem is _____.

5. Select a choice to complete the sentence above that displays the title correctly.

- (A) *Hector the Collector*
- (B) "Hector the Collector"
- (C) <u>Hector the Collector</u>
- (D) None of the above

Richard just wrote a new short story called _____.

6. Select a choice to complete the sentence above that displays the title correctly.

- (A) *My Time in China*
- (B) "My Time in China"
- (C) <u>My Time in China</u>
- (D) None of the above

My cousin's favorite song is _____.

7. Select a choice to complete the sentence above that displays the title correctly.

- (A) *Don't Rain on My Parade*
- (B) "Don't Rain on My Parade"
- (C) <u>Don't Rain on My Parade</u>
- (D) None of the above

Last week, my parents saw the movie _____.

8. Select a choice to complete the sentence above that displays the title correctly.

- (A) *Superman*
- (B) "Superman"
- (C) <u>Superman</u>
- (D) Both A and C

Challenge Yourself!

- **Coordinate Geometry**
- **Writing Titles**

https://www.lumoslearning.com/a/dc5-31

See Page 7 for Signup details

Day 2

1. According to the map, what is the location of the weather station (⚡)?

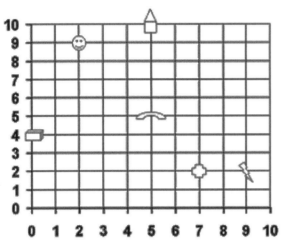

Ⓐ (3,9)
Ⓑ (8,2)
Ⓒ (9,2)
Ⓓ (2,9)

2. According to the map, what is the location of the warehouse (▱)?

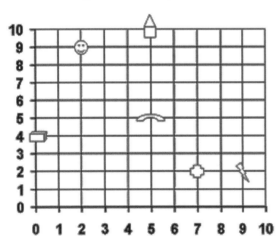

Ⓐ (x = 4)
Ⓑ (0,4)
Ⓒ (y = 4)
Ⓓ (4,0)

3. According to the map, which is located at (7,2)?

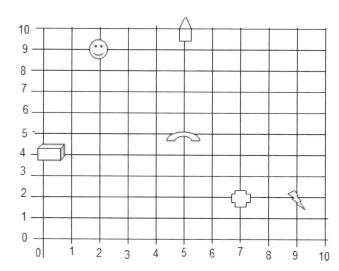

Ⓐ The hospital ✚

Ⓑ The bridge ⌒

Ⓒ The playground ☺

Ⓓ The house 🏠

4. During her run, Lui records the number of minutes it took to reach six mile markers. Based on this graph determine if the statements below are true or false.

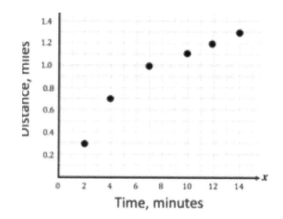

Time, minutes

	True	False
Lui reach mile marker 1.0 in seven minutes.	○	○
It took Lui two minutes to run from mile marker 1.0 to mile marker 1.2.	○	○
Lui ran from mile marker 1.1 to mail marker 1.2 in three minutes.	○	○
Fourteen minutes after Lui started she reached mile marker 1.3.	○	○

Day 2

The birthday party was wonderful! Everyone had so much fun playing and swimming. The birthday presents were great, but my favorite part was the cake. It was incredble!

5. Which word is spelled incorrectly?

- Ⓐ wonderful
- Ⓑ swimming
- Ⓒ favorite
- Ⓓ incredble

I went for a run this morning. Although I usualy run in the evening, I decided to go in the morning because of the weather.

6. Which word is spelled incorrectly?

- Ⓐ morning
- Ⓑ usualy
- Ⓒ decided
- Ⓓ weather

Then, when I came <u>inside</u> to clean, I <u>realized</u> the kitchen sink was <u>clogged</u>, and the washing machine <u>seamed</u> broken.

7. Which underlined word is spelled incorrectly?
Enter your answer in the box given below

Her mother called <u>again</u>, and she could hear the <u>impateince</u> in her voice <u>downstairs</u>. She ran out of her room and <u>leaned</u> over the rail.

8. Which underlined word is spelled incorrectly?
   Enter your answer in the box given below

Challenge Yourself!

- **Real World Graphing Problems**
- **Spelling**

https://www.lumoslearning.com/a/dc5-32

Day 2

See Page 7 for Signup details

Day 3

1. **Complete the following.**
   A plane figure is regular only if it has _____.

   Ⓐ equal sides
   Ⓑ congruent angles
   Ⓒ equal sides and congruent angles
   Ⓓ equal sides, congruent angles, and interior angles that total 180

2. **Complete the following.**
   Two _____ will always be similar.

   Ⓐ circles
   Ⓑ squares
   Ⓒ equilateral triangles
   Ⓓ All of the above

3. **Two interior angles of a triangle measure 30 degrees and 50 degrees. Which type of triangle could it be?**

   Ⓐ a right triangle
   Ⓑ an acute triangle
   Ⓒ an obtuse triangle
   Ⓓ an isosceles triangle

4. **Read the statements below and indicate whether they are true of false.**

	True	False
All squares are rhombuses.	○	○
All parallelograms have four right angles.	○	○
All trapezoids have at least one set of parallel sides.	○	○
All squares are rectangles.	○	○

Day 3

A group of words that expresses a complete thought with a subject and a verb is _____.

5. Select the phrase that best completes the sentence.

- Ⓐ a clause
- Ⓑ an independent clause
- Ⓒ a dependent clause
- Ⓓ a coordinating conjunction

A group of words that does not express a complete thought, but has a subject and a verb is called _____.

6. Select the phrase that best completes the sentence.

- Ⓐ a complete sentence
- Ⓑ an independent clause
- Ⓒ a dependent clause
- Ⓓ a coordinating conjunction

When Juan studied for his quiz at the library.

7. The sentence is an example of _____.

- Ⓐ a complete sentence
- Ⓑ an independent clause
- Ⓒ a dependent clause
- Ⓓ a coordinating conjunction

Miguel loves cars, but he can never find the time to work on one.

8. This is an example of _____.

- Ⓐ a simple sentence
- Ⓑ a compound sentence
- Ⓒ a complex sentence
- Ⓓ an incomplete sentence

Challenge Yourself!

- **Properties of 2D Shapes**
- **Sentence Structure**

https://www.lumoslearning.com/a/dc5-33

Day 3

See Page 7 for Signup details

Day 4

1. Which shape belongs in the center of the diagram?

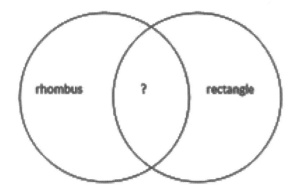

Ⓐ triangle
Ⓑ circle
Ⓒ square
Ⓓ polygon

2. Which shape belongs in section A of the diagram?

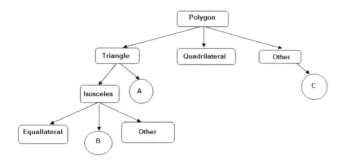

Ⓐ Scalene
Ⓑ Right
Ⓒ Acute
Ⓓ Symmetrical

3. Which shape belongs in section B of the diagram?

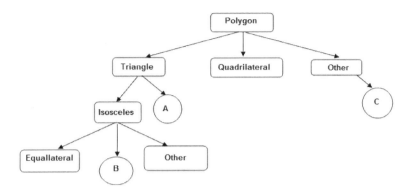

A Scalene
B Isosceles Right
C Acute
D Symmetrical

4. Circle the shape that is a parallelogram with four equal sides and one of the angles measuring 55 degrees

Ⓐ
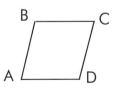

Ⓑ

Ⓒ

Ⓓ

Day 4

Francine: Well, aren't you as refreshing as a cold glass of lemonade on a hot summer day! I'm delighted to meet you! My name is Francine.

Adam: It is a pleasure to make your acquaintance. I am Adam.

5. Based on the dialogue above, which word best describes Francine?

Ⓐ arrogant
Ⓑ friendly
Ⓒ serious
Ⓓ bored

6. Based on the dialogue above, which word best describes Adam?

Ⓐ casual
Ⓑ rude
Ⓒ proper
Ⓓ silly

7. Based on the dialogue above, where do you think Francine might be from?

Ⓐ Europe
Ⓑ Alaska
Ⓒ the South
Ⓓ Canada

8. Which sentence indicates use of dialect?

Ⓐ Would you like for me to help you paint the fence?
Ⓑ Abe thought about it, but he changed his mind.
Ⓒ I reckon I don't have time.
Ⓓ That's ok with me.

Challenge Yourself!

- **Classifying 2D Shapes**
- **Varieties of English**

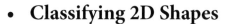
https://www.lumoslearning.com/a/dc5-34

Day 4

See Page 7 for Signup details

Day 5

1. Which of the following number sentences models the Associative Property of Multiplication? Circle the correct answer choice.

   Ⓐ 80 x 5 = (40 x 5) + (40 x 5)
   Ⓑ (11 x 6) x 7 = 11 x (6 x 7)
   Ⓒ 3 x 4 x 2 = 2 x 4 x 3
   Ⓓ 44 x 1 = 44

2. Identify the expression that equals 2?

   Ⓐ [(3 x 2) + 4] ÷ 5
   Ⓑ 2 x [(5 x 4) ÷ 10]
   Ⓒ 12 - [(4 + 8) ÷ 3]

3. Rewrite the equation below substituting a number value for 'a' and an operation for the question mark that would result in a solution of 10.

   20 ÷ [5 - (a ? 9)] = 10

4. **In a drawing class, crayons were distributed to 12 students. Six of the students got packets that had 8 crayons and the other six got packets that had 10 crayons. How many crayons were distributed in all?**

Ⓐ 110
Ⓑ 108
Ⓒ 100
Ⓓ 112

Context Clues (L.5.4.A)

Day 5

The snake <u>slithered</u> across the back porch when my mother chased it with a broom.

5. Select the best definition for the underlined word based on the context clues.

Ⓐ stopped
Ⓑ moved
Ⓒ slept
Ⓓ ate

Our dog <u>gnawed</u> through the rope, allowing him to get loose and leave the backyard.

6. Select the best definition for the underlined word based on the context clues.

Ⓐ stopped
Ⓑ moved
Ⓒ slept
Ⓓ chewed

Jan took one look at the <u>hideous</u> creature and ran away in disgust.

7. Select the best definition of the underlined word based on the context clues.

Ⓐ very ugly and frightful
Ⓑ beautiful but frightful
Ⓒ very happy and excited
Ⓓ very scared and alone

Words that provide the definition of an unknown word explicitly stated in the text are considered
_____.

8. Select the phrase that best completes the above sentence.

Ⓐ inferential context clues
Ⓑ unusual context clues
Ⓒ written context clues
Ⓓ direct context clues

Challenge Yourself!

- **Write and Interpret Numerical Expressions**
- **Context Clues**

https://www.lumoslearning.com/a/dc5-35

Day 5

See Page 7 for Signup details

DOWN: 1. Wisp 2. Shaver 3. Toothpaste 4. Hairdryer 5. Hairbrush 6. Shampoo 7. Bathrobe
ACROSS: 6. Spray 8. Brush 9. Mirror 10. Soap 11. Toothbrush 12. Towel

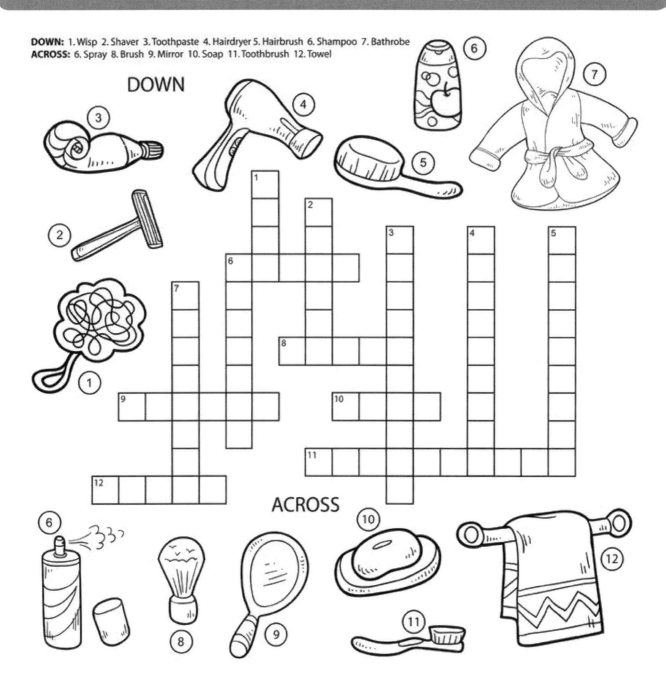

DOWN

ACROSS

Down: 1. Poison 2. Dagger 4. Hat 5. Anchor 6. Rope 9. Hook
10. Sabor 11. Rum 14. Compass 16. Flag 17. Bomb

Across: 3. Map 7. Island 8. Boot 12. Coins 13. Treasure
15. Locket 17. Barrel 18. Spyglass

DOWN

ACROSS

This Week's Online Activities

- **Reading Assignment**
- **Vocabulary Practice**
- **Write Your Summer Diary**

https://www.lumoslearning.com/a/slh5-6

See Page 7 for Signup details

Weekly Fun Summer Photo Contest

Take a picture of your summer fun activity and share it on Twitter or Instagram

Use the **#SummerLearning** mention

@LumosLearning on Twitter or

@lumos.learning on Instagram

Tag friends and increase your chances of winning the contest

Participate and stand a chance to WIN $50 Amazon gift card!

Day 1

Record and Interpret Calculations with Numbers (5.OA.A.2)

1. Olivia had 42 pieces of candy. She kept 9 pieces for herself and then divided the rest evenly among her three friends. Which expression best represents the number of candy each friend received?

   Ⓐ (42 ÷ 3) - 9
   Ⓑ (42 – 9) ÷ 3
   Ⓒ 42 ÷ (9 – 3)
   Ⓓ 42 – (9 ÷ 3)

2. Which is true about the solution to 8 * (467 + 509)?

   Ⓐ It is a number in the ten thousands.
   Ⓑ It is an odd number.
   Ⓒ It is eight times greater than the sum of 467 and 509.
   Ⓓ It is 509 more than the product of 8 and 467.

3. Which is true about the solution to (3,259 – 741) ÷ 3?

   Ⓐ It is one third as much as the difference between 3,259 and 741.
   Ⓑ It is 741 less than the quotient of 3,259 divided by 3.
   Ⓒ It is not a whole number.
   Ⓓ It is a number in the thousands.

4. Each of the 25 students in a class sold 7 items for a fundraiser. Their teacher also sold 13 items. Which expression best represents the number of items they sold in all? Circle the correct answer choice

   Ⓐ 25 x (7 + 13)
   Ⓑ 13 + (25 x 7)
   Ⓒ 7 x (25 + 13)
   Ⓓ 25 + 7 + 13

5. Which of the following is a true statement?

Ⓐ A suffix or ending is an affix, which is placed at the end of a word.
Ⓑ A prefix or beginning is an affix, which is placed at the beginning of a word.
Ⓒ A suffix is attached at the beginning of a word.
Ⓓ Both A and B

6. What is the prefix in the word unhappy?

Ⓐ unh
Ⓑ u
Ⓒ un
Ⓓ None of these

7. What prefix changes the word cycle to mean "a moving device with two wheels?"

Ⓐ tri
Ⓑ dual
Ⓒ bi
Ⓓ quad

8. Identify the root word in the longer word uncomfortable
Enter your answer in the box given below.

Challenge Yourself!

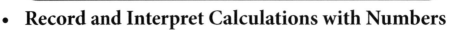

- **Record and Interpret Calculations with Numbers**
- **Roots and Affixes**

https://www.lumoslearning.com/a/dc5-36

Day 1

See Page 7 for Signup details

Day 2

1. Which set of coordinate pairs matches the function table?

Rule: ÷ 3, + 2

Input	Output
9	☐
15	7
27	☐
33	☐

Ⓐ (9 , 1), (15 , 7), (27 , 19), (33 , 25)
Ⓑ (9 , 5), (15 , 7), (27 , 11), (33 , 13)
Ⓒ (9 , 11), (15 , 7), (27 , 29), (33 , 35)
Ⓓ (9 , 15), (15 , 7), (7 , 27), (27 , 33)

2. Which set of numbers completes the function table?

Rule: -4

Input	Output
☐	1
7	3
☐	7
☐	10
☐	15

Ⓐ 0, 3, 6, 11
Ⓑ 3, 10, 17, 25
Ⓒ 4, 28, 40, 60
Ⓓ 5, 11, 14, 19

3. Which set of numbers completes the function table?

Rule: + 1, x 5

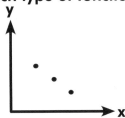

Input	Output
☐	5
2	15
☐	20
☐	35
☐	55

Ⓐ 2, 5, 15, 20
Ⓑ 1, 4, 7, 11
Ⓒ 30, 105, 180, 280
Ⓓ 0, 3, 6, 10

4. Which type of function would result in a graph that looks like this?

Ⓐ One in which x and y increase at fixed rates
Ⓑ One in which x and y decrease at fixed rates
Ⓒ One in which x decreases while y increases
Ⓓ One in which x increases while y decreases

Reference Sources (L.5.4.C)

Day 2

5. If you want to know how to say a word, look at the _____.

Ⓐ guide work
Ⓑ part of speech
Ⓒ pronunciation
Ⓓ definition

Zadey is reading a mystery book.

6. Where would be the best place for her to look up the meaning of a word she doesn't know?

Ⓐ another mystery book
Ⓑ the book's glossary
Ⓒ a thesaurus
Ⓓ a dictionary

marine
Synonyms: sea, saltwater, maritime, oceanic

7. In which source would you find this entry?

Ⓐ a glossary
Ⓑ a book about seas
Ⓒ a dictionary
Ⓓ a thesaurus

8. Fill in the blank by selecting the correct answer from the 4 choices given

You can use a dictionary to learn _____.

Ⓐ correct spellings
Ⓑ definitions
Ⓒ parts of speech
Ⓓ all of the above

Challenge Yourself!

- **Analyze Patterns and Relationships**
- **Reference Sources**

https://www.lumoslearning.com/a/dc5-37

Day 2

See Page 7 for Signup details

Day 3

1. What is the equivalent of 4 and $\frac{3}{100}$?

- Ⓐ 40.3
- Ⓑ 0.403
- Ⓒ 4.03
- Ⓓ 403.0

2. In the number 16,428,095 what is the value of the digit 6?

- Ⓐ 6 million
- Ⓑ 60 thousand
- Ⓒ 16 million
- Ⓓ 600 thousand

3. What is the value of 9 in the number 5,802.109

- Ⓐ 9 thousand
- Ⓑ 9 tenths
- Ⓒ 9 thousandths
- Ⓓ 9 hundredths

4. Which comparison is correct?

- Ⓐ 50.5 = 50.05
- Ⓑ 0.05 = 0.50
- Ⓒ 0.005 = 500.0
- Ⓓ 0.50 = 0.500

5. What is the meaning of the simile below?

The boys ran off like rockets shooting up to the stars.

- Ⓐ The boys ran toward the stars.
- Ⓑ The boys ran away quickly.
- Ⓒ The boys were shooting guns.
- Ⓓ The boys drove rockets.

6. What is the meaning of the metaphor below?

Dad's business is a well-oiled machine.

- Ⓐ Dad's business runs smoothly.
- Ⓑ Dad's business uses a lot of machines.
- Ⓒ Dad's business sells oil.
- Ⓓ Dad's business is putting oil on machines.

7. What is the meaning of the simile below?

My best friend and I are like two peas in a pod.

- Ⓐ The two friends like to eat peas.
- Ⓑ The two friends are very similar.
- Ⓒ The two friends are like vegetables.
- Ⓓ The two friends live in a pod.

8. What is the meaning of the simile below?

Without my glasses, I'm as blind as a bat.

- Ⓐ The person lives in a cave.
- Ⓑ The person is black like a bat.
- Ⓒ The person is blind.
- Ⓓ The person can't see very well without his or her eyeglasses.

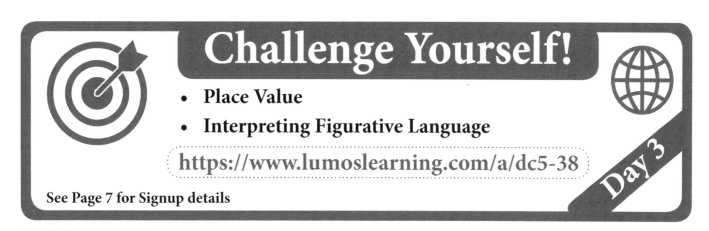

Challenge Yourself!

- **Place Value**
- **Interpreting Figurative Language**

https://www.lumoslearning.com/a/dc5-38

Day 3

See Page 7 for Signup details

1. Astronomers calculate a distant star to be 3×10^5 light years away. How far away is the star?

   Ⓐ 30,000 light years
   Ⓑ 3,000 light years
   Ⓒ 3,000,000 light years
   Ⓓ 300,000 light years

2. A scientist calculates the weight of a substance as $6.9 \div 10^4$ grams. What is the weight of the substance?

   Ⓐ 69,000 grams
   Ⓑ 69 milligrams
   Ⓒ 0.00069 grams
   Ⓓ 6.9 kilograms

3. Looking through a microscope, a doctor finds a germ that is 0.00000082 millimeters long. How can he write this number in his notes?

   Ⓐ 8.2×10^7
   Ⓑ $8.2 \div 10^7$
   Ⓒ 8.2×100.00001
   Ⓓ $8.2 \div 700$

4. Find the missing number.

   _____ x 477 = 47,700,000

   Ⓐ 10,000,000
   Ⓑ 10 x 5
   Ⓒ 10^5
   Ⓓ 1,000

Day 4

5. What is a phrase which contains advice or a generally accepted truth called?

Ⓐ adage
Ⓑ idiom
Ⓒ proverb
Ⓓ simile

Do not put all your eggs in one basket.

6. Which sentence is an example of the above proverb?

Ⓐ Do not put all your golf balls in one game.
Ⓑ Do not keep all your information a secret.
Ⓒ Do not store all your data on just one computer.
Ⓓ Do not eat all your breakfast at dinner.

If anything can go wrong, it will.

7. This famous saying is an example of _____.

Ⓐ an idiom
Ⓑ an adage
Ⓒ a proverb
Ⓓ an alliteration

Remember, don't let the cat out of the bag and tell dad about the surprise party for his birthday.

8. Fill in the blank with a idiom, don't let the cat out of the bag means _____.

Challenge Yourself!

- **Multiplication & Division of Powers of Ten**
- **Idioms, Adages, and Proverbs**

https://www.lumoslearning.com/a/dc5-39

Day 4

See Page 7 for Signup details

1. The number 0.05 can be represented by which fraction?

Ⓐ $\frac{0}{5}$

Ⓑ $\frac{5}{100}$

Ⓒ $\frac{5}{10}$

Ⓓ $\frac{1}{05}$

2. Which of the following numbers is equivalent to one half?

Ⓐ 0.2

Ⓑ 0.12

Ⓒ 1.2

Ⓓ 0.5

3. How is the number sixty-three hundredths written?

Ⓐ 0.63

Ⓑ 0.063

Ⓒ 0.0063

Ⓓ 6.300

4. For which number is this the expanded form?

$9 \times 10 + 2 \times 1 + 3 \times (\frac{1}{10}) + 8 \times (\frac{1}{100})$

Ⓐ 98.08

Ⓑ 93.48

Ⓒ 9.238

Ⓓ 92.38

Day 5

The murmur of the stoves,
The chuckles of the water pipes

5. Choose the set of antonyms of the word murmur.

- Ⓐ roar, growl, loud
- Ⓑ silent, quiet, still
- Ⓒ silent, roar, quiet
- Ⓓ silent, loud, rumble

6. What are synonyms?

- Ⓐ Words that have similar meanings
- Ⓑ Words that have different meanings
- Ⓒ Words that have the same meanings and are spelled the same
- Ⓓ None of the above

7. What are antonyms?

- Ⓐ Words that have the same meanings
- Ⓑ Words that have different meanings
- Ⓒ Both A and B
- Ⓓ Words that have opposite meanings

8. Read the following sentence and identify the words that are antonyms circling the correct option.

There is a huge difference between the lowest and highest scorers of the math exam.

- Ⓐ huge, highest
- Ⓑ lowest, huge
- Ⓒ huge, difference
- Ⓓ lowest, highest

Challenge Yourself!

- **Read and Write Decimals**
- **Synonyms and Antonyms**

https://www.lumoslearning.com/a/dc5-40

Day 5

See Page 7 for Signup details

This Week's Online Activities

- Reading Assignment
- Vocabulary Practice
- Write Your Summer Diary

https://www.lumoslearning.com/a/slh5-6

See Page 7 for Signup details

Weekly Fun Summer Photo Contest

Take a picture of your summer fun activity and share it on Twitter or Instagram

Use the **#SummerLearning** mention

@LumosLearning on Twitter or

@lumos.learning on Instagram

Tag friends and increase your chances of winning the contest

Participate and stand a chance to WIN $50 Amazon gift card!

Week 9 Summer Practice

Day 1

1. Which of the following comparisons is correct?

    Ⓐ 48.01 = 48.1
    Ⓑ 25.4 < 25.40
    Ⓒ 10.83 < 10.093
    Ⓓ 392.01 < 392.1

2. Arrange these numbers in order from least to greatest:
    1.02, 1.2, 1.12, 2.12

    Ⓐ 1.2, 1.12, 1.02, 2.12
    Ⓑ 2.12, 1.2, 1.12, 1.02
    Ⓒ 1.02, 1.12, 1.2, 2.12
    Ⓓ 1.12, 2.12, 1.02, 1.2

3. Which of the following is true?

    Ⓐ 3.21 > 32.1
    Ⓑ 32.12 > 312.12
    Ⓒ 32.12 > 3.212
    Ⓓ 212.3 < 21.32

4. Which of the following numbers completes the sequence below?
    4.17, _____, 4.19

    Ⓐ 4.18
    Ⓑ 4.81
    Ⓒ 5.17
    Ⓓ 4.27

5. Choose the definition of the underlined word in the sentence below.

It is difficult to find a movie store that sells video tapes, because video tapes are nearly <u>obsolete</u>.

Ⓐ very loud and disturbing
Ⓑ simple to operate
Ⓒ no longer produced or used
Ⓓ a traditional story

6. Choose the definition of the underlined word in the sentence below.

If you will <u>provide</u> me with your phone number, I will call you when your order is ready to be picked up.

Ⓐ make available for use
Ⓑ leave one's job and stop working
Ⓒ hold onto
Ⓓ keep secret and confidential

7. Choose the definition of the underlined word in the sentence below.

It is a wise idea to <u>retain</u> a copy of your receipt when making a purchase in case you need to return it.

Ⓐ make available for use
Ⓑ hold onto or keep
Ⓒ throw away or dispose of
Ⓓ make a photocopy

8. Choose the word that correctly completes the sentence below.

The people of the village were tired of being treated badly, so they made the decision to _____ the king.

Ⓐ budge
Ⓑ convert
Ⓒ revert
Ⓓ overthrow

Challenge Yourself!

- **Comparing & Ordering Decimals**
- **Vocabulary**

https://www.lumoslearning.com/a/dc5-41

Day 1

See Page 7 for Signup details

Day 2

1. Which of the following numbers would round to 13.75?

Ⓐ 13.755
Ⓑ 13.70
Ⓒ 13.756
Ⓓ 13.747

2. Jerry spent $5.91, $7.27, and $12.60 on breakfast, lunch, and dinner. About how much did his meals cost in all?

Ⓐ about $24
Ⓑ about $26
Ⓒ about $25
Ⓓ about $27

3. Maria needs to buy wood for a door frame. She needs two pieces that are 6.21 feet long and one piece that is 2.5 feet long. About how much wood should she buy?

Ⓐ about 15 feet
Ⓑ about 9 feet
Ⓒ about 17 feet
Ⓓ about 14 feet

4. A basketball player scores an average of 13.2 points per game. During a 62-game season, he would be expected to score about _____ points. (Assume he will play every game.)

Ⓐ 600 points
Ⓑ 1,000 points
Ⓒ 800 points
Ⓓ 400 points

The Glass Cupboard

There was a king who had a cupboard that was made entirely of glass. It was a special cupboard. It looked empty, but you could always take out anything you wanted. There was only one thing that had to be remembered. Whenever something was taken out of it, something else had to be put back in, although nobody knew why.

One day some thieves broke into the palace and stole the cupboard. "Now, we can have anything we want," they said. One of the thieves said, "I want a large bag of gold," and he opened the glass cupboard and got it. The other two did the same, and they, too, got exactly what they wanted. The thieves forgot one thing. Not one of them put anything back inside the cupboard.

This went on and on for weeks and months. At last, the leader of the thieves could bear it no longer. He took a hammer and smashed the glass cupboard into a million pieces, and then all three thieves fell down dead.

When the king returned home, he ordered his servants to search for the cupboard. When the servants found it and the dead thieves, they filled sixty great carts with the gold and took it back to the king. He said, "If those thieves had only put something back into the cupboard, they would be alive to this day."

He ordered his servants to collect all of the pieces of glass and melt into a globe of the world with all the countries on it, and this was to remind himself and others, to give back something in return when someone shows an act of kindness or gives us something.

5. What happened when the king was away?

Ⓐ There was a storm, and it smashed the glass cupboard.
Ⓑ The people in the palace accidentally broke the glass cupboard.
Ⓒ Some thieves broke into the palace and stole the glass cupboard.
Ⓓ None of the above

6. What did the thieves take out of the cupboard?

Ⓐ They took out bags of gold.
Ⓑ They took out bags of silver.
Ⓒ They took out bags of diamonds.
Ⓓ They took out bags of stones.

7. What did the thieves forget to do?

Ⓐ They forgot to take out everything that was in the cupboard every time.
Ⓑ They forgot to break the cupboard each time they took something out.
Ⓒ They forgot to take out the jewels.
Ⓓ They forgot to put something back each time they took something out.

The Traveler

A weary traveler stopped at Sam's house and asked him for shelter for the night. Sam was a friendly soul. He not only agreed to let the traveler stay for the night; he decided to treat his guest to some curried chicken. So he bought a couple of chickens from the market and gave them to his wife to cook. Then he went off to buy some fruit.

Now Sam's wife could not resist food. She had a habit of eating as she cooked. So, as she cooked the meat, she smelled the rich steam and could not help tasting a piece. It was tender and delicious, and she decided to have another piece. Soon there was only a tiny bit left. Her little son, Kevin, ran into the kitchen. She gave him that little piece.

Kevin found it so tasty that he begged his mother for more. But there was no more chicken left. The traveler, who had gone to have a wash, returned. The woman heard him coming and had to think of a plan quickly. She began to scold her son loudly. "Your father has taught you a shameful and disgusting habit. Stop it, I tell you!" The traveler was curious. "What habit has his father taught the child?" he asked.

"Oh," said the woman, "Whenever a guest arrives, my husband cuts off their ears and roasts them for my son to eat."

The traveler was shocked. He picked up his shoes and fled.

"Why has our guest left in such a hurry?" asked Sam when he came back.

"A fine guest indeed!" exclaimed his wife. "He snatched the chickens out of my pot and ran off with them!"

"The chickens!" exclaimed Sam. He ran after his guest, shouting. "Let me have one, at least; you may keep the other!" But his guest only ran faster!

8. Part A

Why did Sam run after the guest?

- Ⓐ Sam wanted the traveler's ears.
- Ⓑ Sam wanted the traveler's shoes.
- Ⓒ Sam wanted the guest to stay.
- Ⓓ Sam wanted one of his chickens.

8. Part B

Which details in the above paragraph support the fact that the traveler was scared?

(A) The traveler was curious.
(B) The traveler was shocked. He picked up his shoes and fled.
(C) The traveler, who had gone to have a wash, returned.
(D) None of the above.

 **Challenge Yourself!**

- **Rounding Decimals**
- **Supporting Statements**

https://www.lumoslearning.com/a/dc5-42

Day 2

See Page 7 for Signup details

1. **What would be a quick way to solve 596 x 101 accurately?**

   Ⓐ Multiply 5 x 101, 9 x 101, 6 x 101, then add the products.
   Ⓑ Multiply 596 x 100 then add 596 more.
   Ⓒ Shift the 1 and multiply 597 x 100 instead.
   Ⓓ Estimate 600 x 100.

2. **Harold baked 9 trays of cookies for a party. Three of the trays held 15 cookies each and six of the trays held 18 cookies each. How many cookies did Harold bake in all?**

   Ⓐ 297
   Ⓑ 135
   Ⓒ 153
   Ⓓ 162

3. **What's wrong with the following computation?**

   ```
          2 8
        x 5 3
        -------
          3 2
          6 0
        4 0 0
    + 1 0 0 0
      -------
      1 4 9 2
      -------
   ```

   Ⓐ 3 x 8 is multiplied incorrectly.
   Ⓑ 50 x 20 should only have two zeros.
   Ⓒ 5 x 8 is only 40.
   Ⓓ There's a missing 1 that should have been carried from the tens to the hundreds place.

4. **Callie is calculating the product of 268 x 5,321. Help her complete the table below.**

268	×	1	=	268
268	×		=	5,360
	×	300	=	80,400
268	×		=	
	×	**Total**	=	

Do Your Best

Katie stood before the crowd blushing and wringing her hands. She looked out and saw the room full of faces. Some she knew and some she did not, but they were all here to listen to her. Taking a deep breath, she opened her mouth, but no words came out. Tears formed in the corners of her eyes as she closed them.

With her eyes closed, she imagined her mother helping her get dressed and ready for tonight. "Just do your best," is what her mother had told her.

She opened her eyes and found her mother's smiling face in the crowd. Relaxing, she took another deep breath and started singing. She did not stop until she finished, and the crowd was on their feet applauding.

After the show, she found her parents and her friends. They all had wonderful things to say about her song and how proud they were because she kept going even when it seemed like she might give up. She shrugged her shoulders and shared a smile with her mother.

"I just did my best," she answered.

5. The above passage is about _____.

- Ⓐ being determined
- Ⓑ giving up
- Ⓒ listening to friends
- Ⓓ taking a deep breath

6. At the beginning of the story, how was Katie feeling?

- Ⓐ Katie was friendly.
- Ⓑ Katie was excited.
- Ⓒ Katie was depressed.
- Ⓓ Katie was nervous.

7. Part A

At the beginning of the show, what did Katie's friends think she would do?

- Ⓐ Stand there or walk off the stage
- Ⓑ Sing a beautiful song
- Ⓒ Her friends were not paying attention.
- Ⓓ None of the above

Part B
What does the author hope to accomplish in the second paragraph?

Ⓐ The author wants the reader to see how nervous Katie is.
Ⓑ The author wants the reader to see where Katie gets her strength.
Ⓒ The author wants the reader to see why Katie gives up.
Ⓓ The author wants the reader to see how silly Katie is being.

What is this life if, full of care,
We have no time to stand and stare?

No time to stand beneath the boughs
And stare as long as sheep or cows.

No time to see, when woods we pass,
Where squirrels hide their nuts in grass

No time to see, in broad daylight,
Streams full of stars, like skies at night.

No time to turn at Beauty's glance,
And watch her feet, how they can dance.

No time to wait till her mouth can
Enrich that smile her eyes began.

A poor life if, full of care,
We have no time to stand and stare.

-- W. H. Davies

8. What do you think is an appropriate title for the above poem?

Ⓐ "Stand and Stare"
Ⓑ "Leisure"
Ⓒ "Hard Work"
Ⓓ "No Time"

Challenge Yourself!

- **Multiplication of Whole Numbers**
- **Drawing Inferences**

https://www.lumoslearning.com/a/dc5-43

Day 3

See Page 7 for Signup details

Day 4

1. **Which of the following statements is true?**

   Ⓐ $75 \div 0 = 0$
   Ⓑ $75 \div 0 = 1$
   Ⓒ $75 \div 0 = 75$
   Ⓓ $75 \div 0$ cannot be solved

2. **Taylor is putting 100 donuts into boxes. Each box holds 12 donuts. How many donuts will be left over after filling the last box fully?**

   Ⓐ 4
   Ⓑ 8
   Ⓒ 9
   Ⓓ 5

3. **Which of the following statements is true?**

   Ⓐ $26 \div 1 = 1$
   Ⓑ $26 \div 1 = 26$
   Ⓒ $26 \div 1 = 0$
   Ⓓ $26 \div 1$ cannot be solved

4. **Jeremy is rolling coins to take to the bank. He has 680 nickels to roll. If each sleeve holds 40 nickels, how many sleeves will he be able to fill?**

   Ⓐ 8
   Ⓑ 17
   Ⓒ 16
   Ⓓ 12

Day 4

What is this life if, full of care,
We have no time to stand and stare?

No time to stand beneath the boughs
And stare as long as sheep or cows.

No time to see, when woods we pass,
Where squirrels hide their nuts in grass

No time to see, in broad daylight,
Streams full of stars, like skies at night.

No time to turn at Beauty's glance,
And watch her feet, how they can dance.

No time to wait till her mouth can
Enrich that smile her eyes began.

A poor life if, full of care,
We have no time to stand and stare.

- W. H. Davies

5. What is the poet saying in the last stanza of the poem?

Ⓐ This stanza is saying that life is poor even if you have everything, because you have no time to stand and stare.
Ⓑ This stanza is saying that life is not good.
Ⓒ This stanza is saying that there is no time to stand and stare, so life is good.
Ⓓ None of the above

6. Choose a suitable title for this poem.

Ⓐ Life
Ⓑ Stare
Ⓒ Stop and Stare
Ⓓ Life and Stare

My daddy is a tiger,
My mother is a bear
My sister is a pest,
Who messes with my hair
And even though my home,
Is like living in a zoo
I know my family loves me,
And will take care of me too

7. What is this author trying to say in this poem?

Ⓐ Even though the author's family is crazy, they will still take care of each other.
Ⓑ The author's family is too crazy to care.
Ⓒ The author's family is like a bunch of animals.
Ⓓ The author's family is unpredictable.

In the kitchen,
After the aimless

Chatter of the plates,
The murmur of the stoves,

The chuckles of the water pipes,
And the sharp exchanges

Of the knives, forks, and spoons,
Comes the serious quiet

When the sink slowly clears its throat,
And you can hear the occasional rumble

Of the refrigerator's tummy
As it digests the cold.

8. Choose a suitable title for this poem.

Ⓐ "The Sink"
Ⓑ "The Plates"
Ⓒ "The Kitchen"
Ⓓ "The Refrigerator"

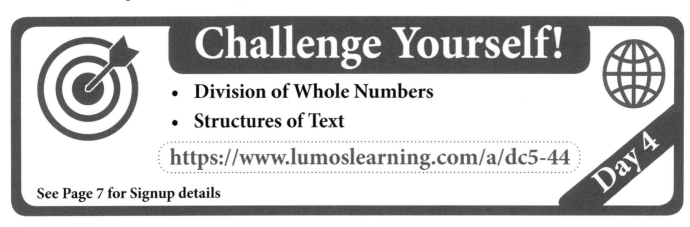

Challenge Yourself!

- **Division of Whole Numbers**
- **Structures of Text**

https://www.lumoslearning.com/a/dc5-44

Day 4

See Page 7 for Signup details

Add, Subtract, Multiply, and Divide Decimals (5.NBT.B.7)

Day 5

1. **Divide 0.42 by 3.**

   Ⓐ 14
   Ⓑ 126
   Ⓒ 0.14
   Ⓓ 12.6

2. **Solve:**
   0.09 ÷ 0.3 =

   Ⓐ 0.27
   Ⓑ 0.003
   Ⓒ 0.027
   Ⓓ 0.3

3. **Circle the number that is 5.47 more than 12.83 + 45.7**

   Ⓐ 68.53
   Ⓑ 62.137
   Ⓒ 64
   Ⓓ 57.9

4. **Solve:**

   12.3 - 1.99 = _____

Late for School

Marrah heard the brakes on the bus as she shoveled the rest of her breakfast into her mouth. "You just missed the bus!" Marrah's mother yelled. "Why can't you ever be on time?"

"I'm sorry, Mom," Marrah sighed. She ran upstairs to her room so she could get her backpack, knowing she needed to hurry because her mother would have to take her to school.

"Let's go, Marrah!" Her mother called from downstairs. "You don't want to be late for school too!"

Frantic now, Marrah lifted her sheets to look under them before dropping to her knees in front of her bed. She pushed mounds of clothes out of the way as she continued to search for her backpack.

"Marrah!" Her mother called again. She could hear the impatience in her mother's voice downstairs. She ran out of her room and leaned over the rail.

"I can't find my backpack!" She cried out.

"You mean this one?" Her mother pulled the bag from the floor beside her.

"Oh," she replied, her shoulders sagging as she walked down the stairs.

"Let's go to school, Marrah." Her mother said with a small smile on her face as they walked out the door.

5. What detail explains that Marrah's mother is kind even when she was frustrated with her daughter? Circle the correct answer choice

Ⓐ Her mother called again and she could hear the impatience in her voice downstairs.

Ⓑ "You just missed the bus!" Marrah's mother yelled. "Why can't you ever be on time?"

Ⓒ "Let's go, Marrah!" Her mother called from downstairs. "You don't want to be late to school too!"

Ⓓ "Let's go to school, Marrah." Her mother said with a small smile on her face as they walked out the door.

THE LITTLE PINK ROSE
Best Stories to Tell to Children (1912)
By Sara Cone Bryant

Once there was a little pink Rosebud, and she lived down in a little dark house under the ground. One day she was sitting there, all by herself, and it was very still. Suddenly, she heard a little tap, tap, tap, at the door. "Who is that?" she said.

"It's the Rain, and I want to come in," said a soft, sad, little voice.

"No, you can't come in," the little Rosebud said. By and by she heard another little tap, tap, tap, on the windowpane. "Who is there?" she said.

The same soft little voice answered, "It's the Rain, and I want to come in!"

"No, you can't come in," said the little Rosebud. Then it was very still for a long time. At last, there came a little rustling, whispering sound, all around the window: rustle, whisper, whisper. "Who is there?" said the little Rosebud.

"It's the Sunshine," said a little, soft, cheery voice, "and I want to come in!"

"N -- no," said the little pink rose, "you can't come in." And she sat still again.

Pretty soon, she heard the sweet little rustling noise at the key-hole. "Who is there?" she said.

"It's the Sunshine," said the cheery little voice, "and I want to come in. I want to come in!"

"No, no," said the little pink rose, "you cannot come in."
By and by, as she sat so still, she heard tap, tap, tap, and rustle, whisper, rustle, all up and down the windowpane, and on the door, and at the key-hole. "Who is there?" she said.

"It's the Rain and the Sun, the Rain and the Sun," said two little voices, together, "and we want to come in! We want to come in! We want to come in!"

"Dear, dear," said the little Rosebud, "if there are two of you, I s'pose I shall have to let you in." So she opened the door a little wee crack, and they came in. And one took one of her little hands, and the other took her other little hand, and they ran, ran, ran with her, right up to the top of the ground. Then they said, --

"Poke your head through!"

So she poked her head through, and she was in the midst of a beautiful garden. It was springtime, and all the other flowers had their heads poked through, and she was the prettiest little pink rose in the whole garden!

6. How can Rosebud best be described in the story?

    Ⓐ She is excited and fearless.
    Ⓑ She is happy and friendly.
    Ⓒ She is shy and scared.
    Ⓓ She is colorful and generous.

7. How can Rosebud best be described in the story?

[answer box]

Late for School

Marrah heard the brakes on the bus as she shoveled the rest of her breakfast into her mouth. "You just missed the bus!" Marrah's mother yelled. "Why can't you ever be on time?"

"I'm sorry, Mom," Marrah sighed. She ran upstairs to her room so she could get her backpack, knowing she needed to hurry because her mother would have to take her to school.

"Let's go, Marrah!" Her mother called from downstairs. "You don't want to be late for school too!" Frantic now, Marrah lifted her sheets to look under them before dropping to her knees in front of her bed. She pushed mounds of clothes out of the way as she continued to search for her backpack.

"Marrah!" Her mother called again. She could hear the impatience in her mother's voice downstairs. She ran out of her room and leaned over the rail.

"I can't find my backpack!" She cried out.
"You mean this one?" Her mother pulled the bag from the floor beside her.
"Oh," she replied, her shoulders sagging as she walked down the stairs.

"Let's go to school, Marrah." Her mother said with a small smile on her face as they walked out the door.

8. In the above story, Marrah appears to be _____ .

- Ⓐ a very disorganized girl
- Ⓑ a very organized girl
- Ⓒ a very punctual girl
- Ⓓ a very disciplined girl

This Week's Online Activities

- **Reading Assignment**
- **Vocabulary Practice**
- **Write Your Summer Diary**

https://www.lumoslearning.com/a/slh5-6

See Page 7 for Signup details

Weekly Fun Summer Photo Contest

Take a picture of your summer fun activity and share it on Twitter or Instagram

Use the **#SummerLearning** mention

@LumosLearning on Twitter or

@lumos.learning on Instagram

Tag friends and increase your chances of winning the contest

Participate and stand a chance to WIN $50 Amazon gift card!

Week 10

Lumos Short Story Competition 2022

Write a short story based on your summer experiences and get a chance to win $100 cash prize + 1 year free subscription to Lumos StepUp + trophy with a certificate.
To enter the competition follow the instructions.

Step 1

Visit **www.lumoslearning.com/a/tg5-6**
and register for online fun summer program.

Step 2

After registration, your child can upload their summer story by logging into the student portal and clicking on **Lumos Short Story Competition 2022.**

Note: *If you have already registered this book and using online resources need not register again. Students can simply log in to the student portal and submit their story for the competition.*
Visit: www.lumoslearning.com/a/slh2022 for more information

Last date for submission is August 31, 2022
Use the space provided below for scratch work before uploading your summer story Scratch Work

Student Name: Nora Moor
Grade: 8

2021 Winning Story

In March 2020, I found out that my 7th-grade exams were canceled. At first, I was excited, but I soon realized that these changes would upend my expectations for school. Over time, my classmates and I realized that the global coronavirus pandemic was not something to be excited about and would have long-lasting effects on our education. My school canceled exams again this year, and, strangely, I found myself missing them. The virus has revealed global inequality regarding health.

Even as America fights the virus, so is it also fighting racism and injustice. The Black Lives Matter movement has shown me how brutal racism can be. The deaths of George Floyd and Breonna Taylor, two African Americans killed by police for no reason, have made me aware of the dangerous injustice in America. Hatred and violence against Asian immigrants are also on the rise. People of color in the US are routinely subjected to prejudice, if not also violence, at the hands of white people. Chinese people are blamed for the "China virus,"; which has led to Asian Americans being attacked. Enduring forms of racism are preventing progress around the world. Racism in society takes many forms, including prejudice, discrimination, and microaggressions. If racism is systemic in America, there will never be true peace or equality until it is uprooted. People see me as a person of color and assume that I'm from Africa because of the color of my skin, even though I am half Black and half white. I don't seem to earn as much respect as a white person would because I am thought of as a foreigner, not a true American. It makes me feel unwelcome and unwanted. I am lucky to have access to technology to keep me engaged in learning. There are still others who don't have the ability to continue learning, whose educational institutions have been shut down by the virus. I have learned that so many people lack access to basic necessities and that racism in America continues to lead to violence and injustice. I aspire to work toward a system that addresses these inequalities in the future. This summer I reflected back on all these things and have learned that no matter what, we all should continue to push on, even through hardships and obstacles.

Submit Your Story Online & WIN Prizes!!!

Student Name: Lillian Olson
Grade: 4

2020 Winning Story

Finding Fun during a Pandemic

This was a weird summer. We did not travel because of COVID-19 and stayed mostly at home and outside around our house. Even when I saw my friends, it was unusual. This summer, I worked and made money helping my parents.

The pandemic allowed me to spend more time inside and I learned many new skills. We made face masks and had to figure out which pattern fits us the best. My sister and I enjoyed creating other arts and crafts projects. Additionally, I have been learning to play instruments such as the piano, guitar, and trombone. We also baked and cooked because we did not go out to eat (at all!). I love baking desserts. The brownies and cookies we made were amazing! I also read for one hour a day and did a workbook by Lumos Learning. I especially loved Math.

Our time outdoors was different this summer. We ordered hens. My family spent a lot of time fixing the coop and setting it up for our 18 chickens. We had a daily responsibility to take care of our chickens in the morning, giving them food and water and in the evening, securing them in their coop. We were surprised that 3 of the hens were actually roosters! Additionally, we exhausted many days gardening and building a retaining wall. Our garden has many different fruits and vegetables. The retaining wall required many heavy bricks, shoveling rocks, and moving dirt around. To cool off from doing all this hard work, we jumped in a stream and went tubing. Our dog, Coco liked to join us.

COVID-19 has also caused me to interact differently with my friends. We used FaceTime, Zoom, and Messenger Kids to chat and video talk with each other. Video chatting is not as fun as being in person with my friends. I love Messenger Kids because it is fun and you can play interactive games with each other.

I had to spend some of my time working. I helped clean my parents' Airbnb. This was busier because of COVID-19. My sister and I will start to sell the chicken eggs once they start to lay which we expect to happen anytime. We had a small business two years ago doing this same thing.

Summer 2020 has been unusual in many ways. We played indoors and outdoors at our house and nearby with family. I have learned new skills and learned to use technology in different ways. Summer of 2020 will never be forgotten!

Submit Your Story Online & WIN Prizes!!!

Answer Key & Detailed Explanations

Week 1

Question No.	Answer	Detailed Explanation
1	A	First, evaluate the numbers within brackets $8 \times 6 = 48$ $8 - 3 = 5$ Now, in step 2, add both the numbers. $48 + 5 = 53$. Hence, A is the correct answer choice.
2	B	Choice A will be $20 - 4 = 16$, while choice b is $12 \div 2 = 6$. Hence, B is the correct answer choice.
3	A	$4 \times (2 + 1) + 6$ $= 4 \times 3 + 6$ $= 12 + 6$ $= 18$ Which is the correct answer. Hence, answer choice A is correct.
4	6	When working with parentheses ( ) and brackets [ ], work from the inside to the outside. First solve the expression in the parentheses. $2 \times [5 - (6 \div 3)] = 2 \times [5 - (2)]$ Next solve the expression in the brackets. $2 \times [5 - (2)] = 2 \times [3]$ Finally, solve the resulting expression. $2 \times [3] = 6$
5	C	In the first stanza, the poet asks a question as shown with the question mark at the end. Beginning in each of the other stanzas the poet begins each one with the phrase "No time." He is telling all of the things that one may not have time to do. However, in the final stanza, the poet answers the question using a statement that begins with "A poor life."
6	D	The word "cunning" means one who is full of tricks. In the beginning of the passage, Tony would be best described as "cautious", because he was trying to prevent the thieves from robbing him. The "well" is just an element in the story that creates the problem. The "thieves" are the villains in the story. At the end, Tony does become clever and outwits the thieves. However, the best title for this story is "The Clever Idea," because it sums up what was done to catch "the thieves" and solve the problem.

Question No.	Answer	Detailed Explanation
7	D	The passage shows that Tony asks his son "to put all of the valuables in the box." The passage does not mention clothes. However, when Tony refers to their valuables, he calls them jewels. Tony also ordered his son to load another box with stones and to throw it into the well. This is the box that the thieves would get while the family's valuables protected.
8 Part A	D	In the first paragraph of the passage, there is direct evidence to the "all of the above" answer, because we know that there has been a severe drought situation. It also introduces the characters Tony, his son, and the thieves. It also states that the thieves have overheard Tony talking with his son about protecting their valuables, so they have a plan to get that box. This becomes the problem that the reader is waiting to be solved.
8 Part B	D	The correct answer is all of the above, because one may conclude from each of the detailed choices in the passage that there was a severe drought, little water in the well, and money was scarce. This is evidence that the country was going through a difficult time.

Question No.	Answer	Detailed Explanation
1	B	First, find the quotient of 72 divided by 8 (72 ÷ 8). Then determine what ten more than that would be (+ 10).
2	D	First, find the product of 12 and 4 (12 x 4). Then subtract this product from 75.
3	A	Show 10 cases of 24 as (10 x 24) and 3 six-packs as (3 x 6). Add the two expressions to find the total: (10 x 24) + (3 x 6).
4 Part A	C	A quick estimate shows that option C, a number in the hundreds times a number in the tens, would result in a number in the thousands. The other options would all result in a number in the hundreds.
4 Part B	D	A quick estimate shows that option D, in which the largest amount is subtracted from 684, would result in the smallest number. Options A and B subtract a relatively small amount from 684, and option C will actually result in a larger number.
5	A	Choice A is correct. There isn't any evidence in the passage to support that the thieves successfully robbed for money, so this answer is incorrect. The thieves did not put the box in the well, but they drew the box out of the well. There is evidence to support the correct answer of how the thieves watered the garden which was by taking water out of the well as they were trying to get to the box.
6 Part A	C	Choice C is correct. The stones were used as a means to divert the robbers to try to remove the box from the well and in that process water the garden. There isn't evidence to support that the stones were valuable to Tony or that it was worth a fortune. In fact there is no money is true but that is not the reason why the box contained stones. The last option is also incorrect.
6 Part B	B	Choice B is correct. Based on the passage above, Tony sent for the soldiers because they enforced the laws. However, there is no direct evidence that Tony trusted the thieves. Also, there isn't any evidence in the passage to indicate that Tony was a member of the Army. The passage does not provide evidence to support the statement that the police were stealing the jewels, because there weren't any police officers present. The soldiers were the "police."

Question No.	Answer	Detailed Explanation
7	A	The evidence shows that this passage is about being determined. The narrator did not give up. She listens to friends and takes a deep breath, but these are the details in the story, not the main idea. Remember that the sum of the details is the main idea which is what the story is mostly about.
8	D	Choice D is correct. The evidence in this story that supports that Katie was nervous at the beginning is her blushing and wringing her hands. There is not enough information in the story to support that Katie was depressed. Do not confuse the crowd's excitement to mean that Katie felt the same way. While at the beginning she was nervous, she seems relieved at the end or glad that it was over. Because Katie had so many people happy for her, one might assume that she was friendly, but there isn't any evidence to support that in the story.

Question No.	Answer	Detailed Explanation
1	B	The rule is multiply by 3, so plugging in each input number results in the following: $1 \times 3 = 3$, $2 \times 3 = 6$, $8 \times 3 = 24$, $12 \times 3 = 36$.
2	C	The rule is add 4, then divide by 2, so plugging in each input number results in the following: $(4 + 4) \div 2 = 4$, $(6 + 4) \div 2 = 5$, $(22 + 4) \div 2 = 13$, $(40 + 4) \div 2 = 22$.
3	A	The rule is multiply by 2, then subtract 1, so plugging in each input number results in the following: $5 \times 2 - 1 = 9$, $9 \times 2 - 1 = 17$, $14 \times 2 - 1 = 27$, $25 \times 2 - 1 = 49$. To create coordinate pairs, write the input number followed by the output number, separated by a comma, in parentheses.
4	-2	The pattern is Add 2, Subtract 5. Since 5 was just subtracted from 6 to get 1, the pattern would continue: 3, -2 . . .
5	C	The evidence in this passage best supports the choice "Do Your Best," because in the end, it was Katie doing her best that allowed her to complete her performance. The rest of the phrases are details of the story, but they are not the main idea, nor do they suggest the most appropriate title. Always remember to choose the best answer. Sometimes, the title will summarize the main idea of the story.
6	B	The overall message of this story is to "Always Do Your Best." The last sentence, "I just did my best," echoes this message. There isn't any evidence to support "closing your eyes...," "giving up under pressure," or "never letting your friends down" as correct answer choices. These are the details that help move the plot of the story along.
7		We learn to never give up. The main character, Katie puts in her best efforts, does not give up and uses encouraging words to get her through. Hence, the lesson that the passage teaches is "Never give up".
8	C	The evidence clearly suggests that the purpose of this story is to show how giving back something in return for something else pays off. There isn't any evidence that shows the reader how to break the glass cupboard, or that this story was about the king. Although the king was mentioned in the story, he is not the main part of the story. Also, it can't be about the importance of gold, because there aren't any details to support its significance.

Question No.	Answer	Detailed Explanation
1	B	The ten thousands place is five places to the left of the decimal, so the 1 is in the ten thousands place.
2	D	The thousandths place is three places to the right of the decimal, so the 6 is in the thousandths place.
3	A	The tenths place is immediately to the right of the decimal. In order to show eight-tenths, use an 8 immediately to the right of the decimal. It is common to use a place-holder 0 in the ones place.
4		

	Yes	No
The 5 in 570.22 is ten times greater than 5 in 456.1.	●	○
The 8 in 2.083 is hundred times less than the 8 in 328.7.	●	○
The 3 in 1.039 is hundred times less than the 3 in 67.3.	○	●
The 2 in 9,523 is thousand times more than the 2 in 45.92	●	○

The 5 in 570.22 is in the hundreds place. The 5 in 456.1 is in the tens place. Thus the 5 in 570.22 is ten times greater than the 5 in 456.1. Statement A is correct.

The 8 in 2.083 is in the hundredths place. The 8 in 328.7 is in the ones place. Thus the 8 in 2.083 is hundred times less than the 8 in 328.7. Statement B is correct.

The 3 in 1.039 is in the hundredths place. The 3 in 67.3 is in the tenths place. Thus the 3 in 1.039 is ten times less than the 3 in 67.3. Statement C is incorrect.

The 2 in 9,523 is in the tens place. The 2 in 45.92 is in the hundredths place. Thus the 2 in 9,523 is thousand times more than the 2 in 45.92. Statement D is correct.

Question No.	Answer	Detailed Explanation
5	B	In the first two paragraphs, the evidence clearly supports Katie and her mother as the main characters. They are key to the plot of the story. The story is mainly about Katie getting ready to perform and her mother's assistance. Katie's father and her friends are minor characters and were present to watch her perform, but they were not the focus of the story.
6	C	Katie's friends and her father , who were in the audience watching Katie's performance, are the secondary or minor characters in this story. The plot is not created around these secondary characters because they do not move the plot along.
7 Part A	B	There is evidence in this story to show that Katie is talented, able to sing, and puts forth a lot of effort into overcoming her fear. However, there is no evidence to support that Katie gave up easily, or was meek and ran away from a difficult situation. The evidence that refutes this is Katie's successful performance and the round of applause and approval that she received from the crowd.
7 Part B	A	The evidence in this story shows that Katie's mother is very supportive, because she had helped her to get ready the night before her singing performance. There is no evidence to show that Katie's mother was not supportive or that she didn't like Katie's singing. In the story, there is no evidence that Katie's mother wanted her to make friends, even though some of Katie's friends were in the audience. We cannot assume anything unless there is supporting evidence in the story.
8	A	Evidence in this story clearly supports that Marrah is very disorganized. Being organized is the opposite, so it isn't correct. There is no evidence to directly support it Marrah is disciplined. However, one can conclude that if she is not able to remain organized, then she is not disciplined enough to do what it takes to keep up with her backpack. Being disorganized causes Marrah to be tardy, whereas, if she were organized, she would be punctual.

Question No.	Answer	Detailed Explanation
1	B	10^3 means 10 x 10 x 10, which equals 1,000. 9 x 1,000 = 9,000. Another way to think of this problem is 9 x 10 = 90, then make sure the number of zeros in the answer matches the number of the exponent (3), which is 9,000.
2	B	10^7 means 10 x 10 x 10 x 10 x 10 x 10 x 10, which equals 10,000,000. Divide 10,000,000 by 100, or move the decimal point to the left (because it is division) two places to get 100,000.
3	A	Since the decimal point in 0.51 is being moved four places to the right, it is being multiplied by 10,000. This number can be shown as 10^4.
4	10^3	To write a multiple of ten as a power of ten, count the number of zeros. Then express the quantity as ten to the power of the number of zeros. 1,000 has three zeros so, as a power of ten, $1,000 = 10^3$
5	A	Choice A is correct. This passage is about Sam's wife who could not resist food. Although she was supposed to feed a guest in their home, a "weary traveler" stopping through, she could not resist eating the chickens that she was supposed to share with the traveler. So, she created a false story to scare the traveler away and blamed the two missing chickens on him. All of these actions support Sam's wife's love of food and her willingness to do anything to hide it.
6 Part A	B	Choice B is correct. The evidence in this story supports that this story is about great things happening when you take a risk. In this case, Rosebud took a risk when she let the Sun and Rain in. There is no significant evidence to support taking the time to do things that you like. The story does not focus on the flowers in the garden or explain the importance of Sun and Rain. If there is no textual support, you should eliminate the choice.
6 Part B	D	The story tells the reader that Rosebud bloomed into a beautiful rose. In this section, there is no evidence that indicates she hid in the garden or her house. However, although it is likely that Rosebud became friends with Sun and Rain there is no direct evidence to support this. We can assume this, but we don't have support from the passage.

Question No.	Answer	Detailed Explanation
7	B	The author or narrator wants to help his mother because he says that she works hard as a nurse. Even though she is gone all day for work, that wasn't the reason the author or narrator wanted to help with the housework. There is no evidence that supports that his reason for helping his mother was based on her being a new mother or because she doesn't like housework.
8	A	The evidence in this story/passage clearly supports that the author/narrator wants to see her/his cousin. There is no direct evidence to support that the author's parents do not like to drive, the author's cousin doesn't like movies, or that the author wants to move to California. Some of this might be true, but we don't have the evidence to support that it is.

Question No.	Answer	Detailed Explanation
1	A	The 4 goes in the hundredths place, which is two places to the right of the decimal. All other places get place-holder zeros.
2	C	The two is immediately to the right of the decimal, so it is in the tenths place. It is read "two tenths."
3	B	The fraction is seven tenths. To show this value in decimal form, use the digit 7 in the tenths place (immediately to the right of the decimal).

4

	True	False
345.3 = three hundred forty-five and three hundredths.	○	●
$900 \times 30 \times 2 \times 4 \times (\frac{1}{10}) \times 7(\frac{1}{100})>$ Nine hundred thirty-two and four hundredths	●	○
$604.2 = 600 \times 4 \times 2 \times (\frac{1}{100})$	○	●
1.805 > One and ninety-two hundredths	○	●

Rewrite each expanded form and number names as a number and compare.

345.3 = 345.03 → So, 1st statement is False

$900 \times 30 \times 2 \times 4 \times (\frac{1}{10}) \times 7 \times (\frac{1}{100}) = \frac{1512000}{1000} = 1512$ is greater than 932.04. So, 2nd statement is True.

$600 \times 4 \times 2 \times (\frac{1}{100}) = \frac{4800}{100} = 48$ is not equal to 604.2. So 3rd statement is False.

One and ninety-two hundredths = 1.92 is greater than 1.805. So, 4th statement is False.

| 5 | B | Although salmon is a favorite of many people, it is not the first event of this story. This first sentence is an introductory statement. So, the first important event is that the fish lay their eggs in the river. However, after the eggs are laid, and the fish hatch, they swim to the ocean and live there for three years. |

Question No.	Answer	Detailed Explanation
6	C	According to the text, after Katie took her second breath, she opened her mouth and sang beautifully. Before she opened her voice, she saw her mom smiling. The other answer choices are incorrect because they refer to what Katie did when she took her first breath
7	B	Answer choice B has the correct order of sentences which demonstrate the order in which Emily prepared, cooked, and ate her brownies.
8	B,D,C,A	According to the evidence in the story, the correct sequence will be

Rosebud heard a strange sound
Rosebud had visitors;
Rosebud let her visitors in;
Rosebud poked her head above ground.

Question No.	Answer	Detailed Explanation
1	A	Since each of the options contains only one non-zero digit (4), compare the place value of the 4 to find the lowest number. 0.04 is the lowest number because the 4 is the furthest to the right of the decimal (in the hundredths place).
2	C	In order to find the greatest number, compare the digit in the highest place value. All of the options have 0 ones, so look to the tenths place. The number with 5 in the tenths place is greater than the numbers with 1 or 2 in the tenths place, no matter what comes next.
3	C	Seven hundredths is written 0.07. In order for a number to be lower, it has to have 0 in the tenths place and a digit lower than 7 in the hundredths place.
4	0.85 0.853 0.921 0.96 1.003 1.03	When comparing decimals, if the numbers do not have the same number of decimal places, add zeros to the end of the number until all numbers have the same number of decimals. Then compare the numbers ignoring the decimal point. 1.003, 0.853, 0.850, 1.030, 0.960, 0.921 – Now all numbers have three decimal points. 1003, 853, 850, 1030, 960, 921 – Ignore the decimal points. 850, 853, 921, 960, 1003, 1030 – Ordered from least to greatest 0.85, 0.853, 0.921, 0.96, 1.003, 1.03 – Decimals ordered from least to greatest
5	C	Both A and B answer choices are correct. The setting of this story takes place in the countryside in Tony's backyard. Some evidence to support this is the presence of a well and fruit trees in a garden
6	B	Choice B is correct. The first sentence begins with "Once, there was a severe drought," which indicates that the story's action happened in the past. The verb "was" also indicates past tense.
7 Part A	A	Choice A is correct. As evidenced in the story, the main setting is located in the garden, because Rosebud's house is located in the garden. You can tell this, because once she let Rain and Sun inside, they ran to the top of the ground. And she found herself in the "midst of a beautiful garden."There was no mention of a zoo, forest or town.

Question No.	Answer	Detailed Explanation
7 Part B	D	Choice D is correct. As evidenced in the sentence, the majority of the dialogue between Rosebud, Rain, and Sun takes place underground (in the garden). Another indication is that it says at the end of the sentence that "...ran with her, right up to the top of the ground." The other sentences contain no clue that would suggest that the action is taking place underground.
8	B	Choice B is correct. If the setting of the story is important to the story, it is usually established at the beginning of the story. However, if it is near the middle or end, it is not as important. The introduction of the setting and characters sets up the story's plot, including the problem that is to be solved.

Day 3

Question No.	Answer	Detailed Explanation
1	B	In order to round to the nearest whole dollar, look to the tenths (dimes) place. In $7.48 there is a 4 in the tenths place, which means round down to $7.00.
2	C	In the number 56.389, there is a 3 in the tenths place. Look to the right to see that 8 means round up. The number becomes 56.4 with no hundredths or thousandths.
3	D	In the number 57.81492, there is a 1 in the hundredths place. To determine whether to round up to 2 or remain 1, look to the digit to the right. A 4 means that the number will round down to 57.81

4

	Round Up	Keep
Round 5.483 to the nearest hundredth.	○	●
Round 6.625 to the nearest tenth.	○	●
Round 77.951 to the nearest one.	●	○
Round 172.648 to the nearest hundredth.	●	○

When rounding, look at the digit to the right of the place to be rounded. If the digit is 5 or more, round to the next digit and drop the digits to the right. If the digit is less than 5, keep the number and drop the digits to the right.

A. When rounding 5.483 to the nearest hundredth, look at the thousands digit. Since the thousandths digit is 3, keep the hundredths digit and drop the numbers to the right. 5.483 rounded to the nearest hundredth is 5.48. KEEP

B. When rounding 6.625 to the nearest tenth, look at the hundredths digit. Since the hundredths digit is 2, keep the tenths digit and drop the numbers to the right. 6.625 rounded to the nearest tenth is 6.6. KEEP

C. When rounding 77.951 to the nearest one, look at the tenths digit. Since the tenths digit is 9, round the ones digit up to 8 and drop the numbers to the right. 77.951 rounded to the nearest one is 78. ROUND UP

D. When rounding 172.648 to the nearest hundredth, look at the thousandths digit. Since the thousandths digit is 8, round the hundredths digit up to 5 and drop the numbers to the right. 172.648 rounded to the nearest hundredth is 172.65. ROUND UP

Question No.	Answer	Detailed Explanation
5	A	Since the definition of a simile is a comparison between two unlike things that uses the words like or as, the phrase that reads: "And even though my home is like living in a zoo" is a simile. However, each of the first three lines of the poem are metaphors. So, there are three metaphors. The answer choices two and four are incorrect and do not apply to the question.
6	C	Choice C is correct because using the definition of a metaphor, which is comparing two unlike things without using the words like, as, or than, is applied three times in the first three lines of the poem. The first thing is compared to the second thing using the word "is"-- My daddy IS a tiger, continuing with lines 2 and 3.
7	A	The expression, "Once in a blue moon" is an idiom, but it is not to be taken literally. It's just a way of expressing something that doesn't happen very often. There is no comparison being made between two unlike things, so choices B and C are incorrect.

8

	a simile	personifica-tion	metaphor
The sea glittered like diamonds under the harsh sun rays.	◯		
The spoon ran away to find a better home.		◯	
The pillow was as soft as cotton.	◯		
The biscuit was a paper weight.			◯

"The sea glittered like diamonds..." is a simile that compares two unlike things, the glittering sea and diamonds, and uses the word "like.

"The spoon ran away to find a better home," is an example of personification because it gives human qualities or characteristics to a non-human object, the spoon. The spoon can't actually run, like a human being, to find a new home.

The pillow is being compared to cotton using "as." To be a metaphor, the words, "as soft as" would need to be removed. There are likely idioms and proverbs using the word pillow or even cotton. You can easily Google them: "pillow idioms" or "pillow proverbs" to find out for yourself.

"The biscuit was a paper weight," is actually a metaphor, because it equates the biscuit with having the same ability as a paper weight, but not literally. By definition, there is no simile, personification, or alliteration.

Week 2

Question No.	Answer	Detailed Explanation
1	B	

```
      7 9
    x 1 4
    ------
      3 6
    2 8 0
      9 0
 +  7 0 0
    ------
  1 1 0 6
```

| 2 | C | This is a multiplication problem, because it is an array of 18 rows with 50 objects in each row. |

```
      5 0
    x 1 8
    ------
        0
    4 0 0
        0
 +  5 0 0
    ------
    9 0 0
```

| 3 | D | |

```
      6 8 0
      x 9 4
    --------
          0
      3 2 0
    2 4 0 0
          0
    7 2 0 0
 + 5 4 0 0 0
    --------
    6 3,9 2 0
```

| 4 | 595,134 | |

```
       321
    × 1854
    ------
      1284      321 x 4
     16050      321 x 50
    256800      321 x 800
    321000      321 x 1000
    -------
    595,134
```

Question No.	Answer	Detailed Explanation
5	C	A conclusion to a passage is usually found at the end. Choices A and B are not logical. A passage does not have a conclusion in the beginning or in the middle. Putting the end in the beginning or middle changes the flow and may confuse the reader. However, every passage usually has an ending, so choice D does not make sense.
6	A	The first stanza of the poem is asking a question, while the last stanza answers the question. However, none of the stanzas introduce life or the author. The stanzas are describing things that an individual with a busy life may not have time to do.
7	B	W. H. Davies wrote this poem, and his name is printed at the bottom of the poem. Since there is an author, the other choices are incorrect.
8	D	When you read a humorous piece of writing, you laugh. You would not generally cry (unless you were just laughing so hard that tears welled up in your eyes), or take things seriously, because the laughter may be because of a joke. You would not write down notes during laughter unless of course you are writing down something that was so funny that it made a large audience laugh, and you just wanted to remember what it was.

Question No.	Answer	Detailed Explanation
1	A	The equation 48 ÷ ___ = 12 can be thought of as 48 ÷12 = ___. There are 4 twelves in 48. Check the work by using multiplication (4 x 12 = 48).
2	C	To solve the problem, divide 72 by 8. 72 can be divided evenly by 8. Check the work by using multiplication (8 x 9 = 72).
3	B	1248 divided by 6 is 208 with remainder 0 = 208 R 0 = 208 0/6

Show Work:

```
        0 2 0 8
    6 | 1 2 4 8
        0
        ---
        1 2
        1 2
        ---
          0 4
          0
          ---
            4 8
            4 8
            ---
              0
```

Question No.	Answer	Detailed Explanation
4	C	To find the number that completes the equation, divide 564 by 47. $564 \div 47 = 12$

```
      12
47)564
   47        47 x 1
   9
   94        47 x 2
   0
```

Question No.	Answer	Detailed Explanation
5	C	If this story were told from Marrah's mother's point of view, it would clearly show more of her mother's frustration with Marrah being late and not being able to find things, whereas the point of view that it's written from depicts Marrah's frustration over misplacing her backpack, missing the bus, and being late for school. Since Marrah is telling the story, the reader likely connects better with her. If her mother were telling the story, the reader might make a connection with the mother..

Question No.	Answer	Detailed Explanation
6	A	The points of view are first, second, third, limited omniscient, and omniscient. However, the first person point of view is powerful and engaging because the author is telling the story in his or her own words. The words describe the action. It also uses the first person pronouns: I, me, and my. He and she are used with the third person point of view, while you is used in second person point of view. In omniscient, the narrator knows the thoughts and feelings of all of the characters and is outside of the action, while limited omniscient is when the narrator knows the thoughts and feelings of some of the characters.
7		If the Sun was telling the story, it would focus on his excitement about helping Rosebud. The evidence that supports this is that he was anxious to get in Rosebud's house, and when she let the Rain and him in, they took her hands and ran off with her so that she could discover how beautiful she was.

8

	First Person	Third Person
While we were walking together, I lost my dog.	◯	
Kelsey was extremely upset. While she and Danny were together, he got lost.		◯
This is the first time we have had a chance to go to the zoo.	◯	

The first sentence, which uses the pronouns we and I, is written in first person point of view.

The second sentence, which uses the name Kelsey, Danny, and the pronouns she and he, is written from the third person point of view.

The third sentence, which uses the plural pronoun we, is written in first person point of view.

Question No.	Answer	Detailed Explanation
1	A	Add each number, maintaining the place value of the digits. Any time a sum exceeds 9, carry the tens to the next highest place value.

$$
\begin{array}{r}
4.1\,8 \\
3.7\,5 \\
+\ 3.9\,9 \\
\hline
1\,1.9\,2 \\
\hline
\end{array}
$$

| 2 | C | Add each number, maintaining the place value of the digits. |

$$
\begin{array}{r}
6.4\,7\,2 \\
0.0\,1 \\
3 \\
+\ 0.5 \\
\hline
9.9\,8\,2 \\
\hline
\end{array}
$$

| 3 | B | Add each number, maintaining the place value of the digits. Any time a sum exceeds 9, carry the tens to the next highest place value. |

$$
\begin{array}{r}
2.0\,9 \\
2.0\,9 \\
3.7\,2 \\
+\ 6.6\,0 \\
\hline
1\,4.5\,0 \\
\hline
\end{array}
$$

| 4 | 0.25 | To solve, use division. Move both decimal places to the right one place, so you are dividing by a whole number (0.5 ÷ 2). Since 5 will not divide evenly by 2, think of it as 0.50. Divide the numbers without the decimal point. Then, insert a decimal into the answer, leaving the same number of places to the right of the decimal as the dividend (remember that you used 0.50, so there should be two places to the right of the decimal in your answer). |

$50 \div 2 = 25 \rightarrow 0.25$

Question No.	Answer	Detailed Explanation
5	B	Without the illustration, the reader might assume that Eliza is describing her experience of an actual train ride. So without this, the reader may be confused, but the author doesn't appear to be confused. Since the first sentence opens with a "winding train," this does not support the choice of a car. There isn't evidence of roads, highways, or other cars.
6	A	Media uses sounds, images, and language to convey a message, while text relies on the use of words to get a message across. Movies are considered a form of media. Verbs help to describe the action. Similes, metaphors, and alliteration are figures of speech that are used in both media and text..
7 Part A	D	As a visual aide, the illustration clearly shows that Tommy is thinking about a hat when he uses the word top. Without the illustration, a reader might visualize a top as being a shirt or something to cover the part of the body above the waist, rather than a type of hat
7 Part B	A	Without the illustration, the reader might assume that a top refers to a shirt. In different regions or parts of the world, a different word may be used to describe a common thing. For example, the words soda, soda pop, pop, drink, and "a coke" all refer to something to drink or to quench thirst.
8	D	In informational text, a bar graph works best as a visual aid. Text only means there are no images used, only words. An illustration may be more appropriate for fictional text. The Internet link may link the reader to appropriate illustrations or visual aids, but the Internet link is not a visual aid

Week 3

Question No	Answer	Detailed Explanation
1	B	When fractions have a common denominator (in this case 10), just add the numerators (2 + 1 = 3) and keep the denominator the same.
2	A	Add the whole numbers (1+1) to get 2. Then add the fractions. As they have a common denominator of 4, just add the numerators (1+2) to get $\frac{3}{4}$. The total is $2\frac{3}{4}$
3	B	As the fractions have a common denominator of 4, just subtract the numerators (3 - 2) to get 1/4.
4	$\frac{11}{35}$	When subtracting fractions, first get a common denominator. The lowest common denominator of 5 and 7 is 5 X 7 = 35. Write an equivalent expression with denominators of 35 and subtract numerators. $\frac{3}{5} - \frac{2}{7} = \frac{21}{35} - \frac{10}{35} = \frac{11}{35}$
5	B	Personification is giving human characteristics to non-human things. In the first poem, Beauty is personified and in the second poem the appliances and utensils in the kitchen are personified
6	B	When comparing two texts to determine if they are like or different, one should look at the type, style, and purpose of the text. These are the various aspects of text that create the content
7	B	According to the chart, the two months with the highest book check outs are September and October. The evidence in the chart shows that these two months are above 600 while the months of November and December are below 600.
8	D	According to the chart, students borrowed a total of 475 books during the month of December, which was the lowest number

Day 3

Question No.	Answer	Detailed Explanation
1	C	Multiply 60 (the number of minutes in an hour) by 3/4 to find the number of minutes she practiced.

$$60 \times \frac{3}{4} = \frac{180}{4}$$

$$= 45$$

| 2 | A | Multiply 30 by 3/5 to find the number of boys. |

$$30 \times \frac{3}{5} = \frac{90}{5}$$

$$= 18$$

If there are 18 boys, there must be 12 girls (30 - 18 = 12).

| 3 | D | To solve, divide 11 miles by 3 hours. Convert the improper fraction to a mixed number. |

$$\frac{11}{3} = 3\frac{2}{3}$$

4

	>	<	=
$\frac{5}{6} - \frac{2}{3} \;\square\; \frac{1}{2} - \frac{3}{8}$	●	○	○
$\frac{5}{6} + \frac{2}{3} \;\square\; \frac{3}{4} + \frac{5}{12}$	●	○	○
$\frac{3}{15} + \frac{2}{5} \;\square\; \frac{1}{3} + \frac{2}{5}$	○	●	○
$\frac{7}{8} - \frac{1}{4} \;\square\; \frac{3}{4} - \frac{1}{8}$	○	○	●

Question No.	Answer	Detailed Explanation
4 Contd.		When adding or subtracting fractions first get a common denominator, then add or subtract the numerators and simplify the answer. When comparing fractions get a common denominator and compare numerators.

$$\frac{5}{6} - \frac{2}{3} = \frac{5}{6} - \frac{4}{6} = \frac{1}{6} \; ; \; \frac{1}{2} - \frac{3}{8} = \frac{4}{8} - \frac{3}{8} =$$

$$\frac{1}{8} \rightarrow \frac{1}{6} > \frac{1}{8} \text{ because } \frac{8}{48} > \frac{6}{48}$$

$$\frac{5}{6} + \frac{2}{3} = \frac{5}{6} + \frac{4}{6} = \frac{9}{6} = \frac{3}{2} \; ; \; \frac{3}{4} + \frac{5}{12} = \frac{9}{12} + \frac{5}{12}$$

$$= \frac{14}{12} = \frac{7}{6} \rightarrow \frac{3}{2} > \frac{7}{6} \text{ because } \frac{9}{6} > \frac{7}{6}$$

$$\frac{3}{15} + \frac{2}{5} = \frac{3}{15} + \frac{6}{15} = \frac{9}{15} = \frac{3}{5} \; ; \; \frac{1}{3} + \frac{3}{5} = \frac{5}{15} + \frac{9}{15}$$

$$= \frac{14}{15} \rightarrow \frac{3}{5} < \frac{14}{15} \text{ because } \frac{9}{15} > \frac{14}{15}$$

$$\frac{7}{8} - \frac{1}{4} = \frac{7}{8} - \frac{2}{8} = \frac{5}{8} \; ; \; \frac{3}{4} - \frac{1}{8} = \frac{6}{8} - \frac{1}{8}$$

$$= \frac{5}{8} \rightarrow \frac{5}{8} = \frac{5}{8}$$

Question No.	Answer	Detailed Explanation
5	A	In this passage, the writer implies that Mrs. Davis is a wealthy woman. The following pieces of evidence are clues that she is wealthy: "great big apartment on the top floor," "fine, leather furniture," "expensive works of art," and "silk robe."
6	A	Dr. Thomas is visiting Mrs. Davis, because she had been sick. The following clues from the passage help readers make this inference: Mrs. Davis was in bed. Dr. Thomas commented that she seems to be feeling better, which implies that she had been sick.
7	B	Choice B is correct. Choice A is incorrect, because the paragraph does not mention a husband. Choice C is incorrect, because the paragraph does not imply that Kara's mother is tired. Choice B is correct, because there is evidence in the paragraph that Kara's mother is hard-working such as the fact that she wakes up early to study, works at a job during the day, takes college classes at night, and volunteers on the weekends.
8	D	Readers do all of these behaviors when they read, helping them to make inferences or draw conclusions. This is called "reading between the lines."

Question No.	Answer	Detailed Explanation
1	A	The first three cookies can be shared by having each friend receive 1 whole cookie. That leaves 1 cookie to be divided among the three friends. This can be shown as a fraction with the dividend (1) as the numerator and the divisor (3) as the denominator. Each friend will receive 1 whole cookie and $\frac{1}{3}$ of the last cookie that was divided.
2	B	The number 5 goes into 18 three whole times (5 x 3 = 15), leaving a remainder of 3. That three can be divided by 5 to get the required fraction, $\frac{3}{5}$.
3	B	To solve, divide 90 minutes by 4 squads. This creates the improper fraction $\frac{90}{4}$. To change it to a mixed number, divide 90 by 4 to get 22 remainder 2. The remainder of 2 also needs to be divided among the 4 squads, so it becomes the fraction $\frac{2}{4}$, or $\frac{1}{2}$. Each squad will play for $22\frac{1}{2}$ minutes.
4		Divide 6-feet by 8 or write $\frac{6}{8}$. Then simplify the fraction $$\frac{6}{8}=\frac{\frac{6}{2}}{\frac{8}{2}}=\frac{3}{4}$$ Therefore each bracelet was $\frac{3}{4}$-feet long.
5	A	In the first paragraph, the author provides specific details of how the orange has been dispersed all over the world and as one of the most important internationally traded products, it now grows in the warmer parts of the world. We don't have evidence about how the ancient Romans and Greeks knew about oranges. There is also no information to support how oranges were traded.
6	D	According to the second sentence of the first paragraph, oranges are grown in most of the warmer parts of the world.
7	C	The fact that when someone touches an orange, they are not touching the fleshy part until the skin is peeled, and the orange's thick, oily, bitter skin protects it from insects, makes the orange a clean fruit, according to the passage
8	D	According to the first sentence of the second paragraph, the passage is about the types of oranges and their usefulness and where they are grown.

Question No.	Answer	Detailed Explanation
1	A	First, multiply the numerators (2 x 4 = 8) then multiply the denominators (3 x 5 = 15) to get the fraction 8/15.
2	D	Multiply the first two terms first, using $\frac{5}{1}$ for the whole number 5. $\frac{5}{1} \times \frac{2}{3} = \frac{10}{3}$. Then multiply this fraction by the third term: $\frac{10}{3} \times \frac{1}{2} = \frac{10}{6}$ Change the improper fraction $\frac{10}{6}$ to a mixed number by dividing 10 by 6. Then change $1\frac{4}{6}$ into lowest terms, which is $1\frac{2}{3}$.
3	B	Multiplying a fraction by a whole number is the same as multiplying the numerator by a whole number then dividing the product by the denominator.
4		When multiplying fractions, multiply numerators and put them over the product of the denominators. Then simplify the fraction.

$\frac{1}{6}$	×	$\frac{3}{4}$	=	$\frac{3}{24}$	=	$\frac{1}{8}$

5	C	Choice C is correct. In the first sentence of the second paragraph, it says that "thieves broke into the palace." They did this while the king was away. We know that the king was away, because in a later paragraph it said "when the king returned." Someone has to go away before they can return.
6	B	Choice B is correct. The reason that the king wanted a globe with all the countries of the world upon it was to remind himself to give back something when someone gives him something or does something for him. The passage states this in the last paragraph.
7 Part A	C	Choice C, she relaxed and started singing, is correct. When Katie closed her eyes and remembered what her mother had said, it comforted her and gave her the courage she needed to sing her song. Choice A is incorrect, because she blushed and wringed her hands before she closed her eyes and remembered what her mother had said to her. Choice B is incorrect, because it did not happen in the passage.
7 Part B	B	Choice B, her parents and friends told her they were proud of her, is the correct choice. The passage says that this happened after Katie's singing performance. Choice A is incorrect, because the opposite happened. Katie didn't give up. Choice C is incorrect, because her mother helped her get dressed and ready before the performance. "As a result" means "What happened after" something else happened.

Question No.	Answer	Detailed Explanation
8 Part A	D	Choice D is correct. In the very first sentence of the passage, it says that Marrah was eating breakfast when the bus stopped at her house. We don't know the reason why she hadn't finished her breakfast yet, but we know that is why she missed the bus. Choice B is incorrect, because we can assume that Marrah was already dressed when she was eating breakfast. Choice C is incorrect, because she hadn't realized that she didn't know where her backpack was at the time she missed the bus.
8 Part B	A	Choice A is correct. In the third paragraph, it says that Marrah ran upstairs to her room to get her backpack. When she got to her room, she couldn't find it so she started looking. She looked under her sheets and under mounds of clothes. Choice B is incorrect, because she had already missed the bus. That's not why she was searching in her room. Choices C and D are incorrect, because they did not happen in the story.

Question No.	Answer	Detailed Explanation
1	A	Find the area of the desk top by multiplying: 7/8 yd x ¾ yd = 21/32 yd²
2	C	Find the area of the floor by multiplying: 2 ½ x 3 ¾ = 5/2 x 15/4 = 75/8 = 9 3/8
3	D	Multiplying length x width of a rectangle and tiling the rectangle with unit squares are both accurate ways to determine area. Therefore, Lin and Tyra should both end up with the same answer, or nearly the same answer (since counting fractional parts of tiles isn't as precise as multiplying).
4	$1\frac{2}{3}$	The area of a rectangle is equal to the length multiplied by the width. $\text{Area} = 2 \times \frac{5}{6} = \frac{2}{1} \times \frac{5}{6} = \frac{2 \times 5}{1 \times 6} = \frac{10}{6} = \frac{\frac{10}{2}}{\frac{6}{2}} = \frac{5}{3} = 1\frac{2}{3}$
5	A	A reference source is a set of information that an author can base an article or story on. Almanacs, newspapers, and interviews are references to sources. One usually cannot check references out from the library. However, many of the same resources are accessible online. References contain different kinds of information. The reference source is not the information but it is the location of the information that is gathered to write a report.
6	B	With respect to language, the "prompt" is generally given in the form of a question. There may be many ways to answer the question. However, its purpose is not to tell you exactly what a paper is about, but to give you a basic idea of what to write about. If the "prompt' is for an essay, the essay will still have the three basic parts, which are the introduction, body, and conclusion.
7	D	The reader can use the context clues around the word "hatch". The meaning of the word "hatch" in this context refers to fish breaking out of the eggs and filling the pool.
8	C	The reader can look at the parts of the word aftermath, "after" is a clue that it's referring to what happened after the volcanos (erupted). So, the best answer is consequences. You can test the word when you substitute consequences for the word aftermath, and the meaning of the sentence is similar. The words aftermath and consequences both mean that something is a result of something else that happens. The word cause can be used in the sentence and the sentence still sounds the same, the words cause and aftermath are not the same.

Question No.	Answer	Detailed Explanation
1	A	When multiplying two numbers ('a' and 'b'), the product will be 'a' times as much as 'b' or 'b' times as much as 'a'.
2	C	When multiplying, if one factor is a fraction greater than 1, the product will be greater than the other factor.
3	B	When multiplying, if one factor is a fraction less than 1, the product will be less than the other factor.

4

$\frac{8}{9}$	×	**<1**	<	$\frac{8}{9}$
<1	×	$1\frac{1}{5}$	<	$1\frac{1}{5}$
$\frac{5}{4}$	×	**>1**	>	$\frac{5}{4}$

A whole number or fraction multiplied by a fraction less than one results in a value less than the original number. A whole number or fraction multiplied by a fraction greater than one results in a value greater than the original number.

A. Since the result is a number less than $\frac{8}{9}$, the fraction entered must be less than one.

B. Since the result is a number less than $1\frac{1}{5}$, the fraction entered must be less than one.

C. Since the result is a number greater than $\frac{5}{4}$, the fraction entered must be greater than one

Question No.	Answer	Detailed Explanation
5	C	The index of a text, usually found at the back of a book, is a sequential listing of topics with page numbers. Rather than reading the entire book, sometimes a student only needs to gather information about a specific topic, so the index will help a student to locate specified information quickly.
6	B	The glossary is a specialized dictionary inside of a particular text that explains difficult words. It is very helpful because it is quick and provides the definition as it relates to the text. A dictionary may have more meanings, and it may be difficult to select the definition that applies to the usage of the word that is encountered. This could cause one to misinterpret the content if wrong meaning of a word or phrase is chosen.

Question No.	Answer	Detailed Explanation
7	D	Since the passage has factual information, it is considered to be a work of nonfiction. It provides information. Realistic fiction is a story that requires the use of characters and has a plot that is actually false but is based on real people, events, and places.
8	A	When writing a report about the aftermath of volcanoes, using the cause and effect text structure will explain the causes of volcanoes, and then the aftermath or the result of the volcanoes. Because the volcanoes (erupted), damaged homes and lost lives were the aftermath or the result of what happened

Question No.	Answer	Detailed Explanation
1	A	Multiplying a number by a fraction less than 1 will result in a product that is less than the original number.
2	D	Multiplying a number by a fraction greater than 1 will result in a product that is greater than the original number.
3	B	Multiplying a number by a fraction greater than 1 will result in a product that is greater than the original number. Since the second factor is only 1/7 more than one, the product will be just slightly greater than 18,612. 18,612 x 1/7 = 21,270.86
4	$\frac{4}{3}$	Multiplying a number by a fraction greater than 1 will result in a product that is greater than the original number. Since the product is only slightly greater than the original number, the other factor will be just slightly greater than 1. Therefore, $\frac{4}{3}$ (which is equal to $1\frac{1}{3}$) is the only option possible.
5	C	This paragraph was written in the 3rd person point of view, because the author was not in the story. It was told from an observer's point of view. We know this, because the characters (Mary and Peter) are named. If it was told from the 1st person point of view, the pronoun "I" would be used. If it was told in the 2nd person point of view, it would use the pronoun "you."
6	C	This paragraph was written in the 3rd person point of view, because the author was not in the story. It was told from an observer's point of view. We know this, because the character (Lucy) is named. If it was told in the 1st person point of view, the pronoun "I" would be used. If it was told in the 2nd person point of view, it would use the pronoun "you.
7	A	This passage was written in the 1st person point of view. The author is one of the characters in the story. The author is the person visiting Mrs. Davis. We know this, because the pronouns "I" and "me" are used.
8	C	The paragraph was written in the 3rd person point of view, because the author was not in the story. It was told from an observer's point of view. We know this, because the character (Vince) is named. If it was told in the 1st person point of view, the pronoun I would be used. If it was told in the 2nd person point of view, it would use the pronoun "you." When Vince called back to the employee stating that he would have the muffins ready in ten minutes, he used the pronoun "I," but it was used in dialogue. The author was reporting what he said. So this does not mean it was in the 1st person point of view.

Question No.	Answer	Detailed Explanation
1	A	To multiply a whole number by a fraction, represent the whole number as $\frac{17}{1}$. Then, multiply numerators ($17 \times 3 = 51$) to find the numerator and multiply denominators ($1 \times 4 = 4$) to find the denominator. Change the improper fraction $\frac{51}{4}$ to a mixed number by dividing 51 by 4 to equal $12\frac{3}{4}$.
2	A	To find how far the teammates ran, subtract $\frac{3}{5}$ (Carl's distance) from $\frac{5}{5}$ (the total distance) to get $\frac{2}{5}$. Then, multiply this fraction by the distance of the race. Multiply numerators ($2 \times 9 = 18$) to find the numerator and multiply denominators ($5 \times 10 = 50$) to find the denominator. Reduce the fraction $\frac{18}{50}$ to $\frac{9}{25}$.
3	B	To multiply a whole number by a mixed number, first change the whole number to a fraction ($\frac{3}{1}$) and change the mixed number to a fraction ($\frac{9}{5}$). Multiply numerators ($3 \times 9 = 27$) to find the numerator and multiply denominators ($1 \times 5 = 5$) to find the denominator. The improper fraction $\frac{27}{5}$ can be changed to the mixed number $5\frac{2}{5}$
4	4 miles	To find how far Riley ran, multiply 6 by $\frac{2}{3}$. When multiplying a whole number by a fraction rewrite the whole number as a fraction with a denominator of 1. Then multiply the numerators and denominators. Finally simplify the answer to a fraction in simplest form or a mixed number. $6 \times \frac{2}{3} = \frac{6}{1} \times \frac{2}{3} = \frac{12}{3} = 4$
5	D	Information about W. H. Davies, the author of the poem, can be found in the library, on the Internet, or in a book about different poets. All of the resources have a variety of information that can provide information about the poet
6	C	Information from the passage may be found in a personal journal or diary, because it includes information that is relevant to the author, which may be considered in some cases opinions, rather than facts. Factual information is generally found in newspaper articles, unless it's an editorial, and also on the Internet or in a book report.

7

In the front of a textbook, the Table of Contents lists the chapters in the textbook. You would locate the title Civil War and the page number.

A glossary is a textbook specific dictionary that has some of the words or phrases that might be difficult to understand, like the definition of a key word.

The back of a book often has on index, which is an alphabetical listing of important topics covered in the book with page numbers.

If you are looking for when (and where) a book was published, you can locate that information on the copyright page found in the front of the book.

	Table of Contents	glossary	Index	copyright page
where would you look to locate a chapter on the Civil War	●			
where would you look to locate the definition of a key word		●		
where would you look to locate the alphabetical list of important topics			●	
where would you look to locate when the book was published				●

8 **A**

Choice A is correct. The appendix is located in the back of a textbook and contains extra charts, graphs, and maps. Unless you are looking for a specific topic, chapter, or definition of a word, the other choices will not be helpful.

Question No.	Answer	Detailed Explanation
1	D	The first step in dividing by a fraction is to find its reciprocal, which is the reverse of its numerator and denominator. The fraction 1/3 becomes 3/1, or the whole number 3. Then solve by multiplying. 2x3=6.
2	A	The first step in dividing by a fraction is to find its reciprocal, which is the reverse of its numerator and denominator.
3	D	The first step in dividing by a fraction is to find its reciprocal, which is the reverse of its numerator and denominator. The fraction 2/3 becomes 3/2. Then solve by multiplying (use 3/1 for the whole number 3): 3/1 X 3/2 = 9/2 = 4 1/2.

4

	True	False
$6 \div \dfrac{1}{3} > 16$	●	
$\dfrac{1}{4} \div 3 =$		●
$12 \div \dfrac{1}{6} < 80$	●	
$\dfrac{1}{5} \div 2 > 9$		●

To divide a number by a fraction, multiply the number by the reciprocal of the fraction.

A. $6 \div \dfrac{1}{3} = \dfrac{6}{1} \times \dfrac{3}{1} = \dfrac{18}{1} = 18$ Since 18>16, $6 \div \dfrac{1}{3} > 16$ is a true statement.

B. $\dfrac{1}{4} \div 3 = \dfrac{1}{4} \div \dfrac{3}{1} = \dfrac{1}{4} \times \dfrac{1}{3} = \dfrac{1}{12}$ Since $\dfrac{1}{12} \neq \dfrac{3}{12}$, $\dfrac{1}{4} \div 3 = \dfrac{3}{12}$ is a false statement.

C. $12 \div \dfrac{1}{6} = \dfrac{12}{1} \div \dfrac{1}{6} = \dfrac{12}{1} \times \dfrac{6}{1} = \dfrac{72}{1} = 72$ Since 72<80, $12 \div \dfrac{1}{6} < 80$ is a true statement.

D. $\dfrac{1}{5} \div 2 = \dfrac{1}{5} \div \dfrac{2}{1} = \dfrac{1}{5} \times \dfrac{1}{2} = \dfrac{1}{10}$ Since $\dfrac{1}{10} < 9$, $\dfrac{1}{5} \div 2 > 9$ is a false statement.

Question No.	Answer	Detailed Explanation
5	D	Choice D is correct. Both paragraphs two and three refer to types and details of oranges.
6	D	The first sentence of the last paragraph states that oranges have many medicinal values. Since this refers to caring for one's health, this paragraph discusses the health benefits of oranges.
7	B	According to the graph, the color of the highest bar in the middle represents mandarin oranges
8	C	Evidence for supporting details found in the text, includes charts, illustrations, graphs, and headings

Question No.	Answer	Detailed Explanation
1	B	Division can be checked by multiplying the quotient by the divisor to equal the dividend. In this case, $24 \times \frac{1}{4} = \frac{24}{4} = 6$.
2	D	In option D, each of four units is divided into thirds, resulting in a total of 12 units. Option B also produces 12 units, but it shows 3 units divided into fourths.
3	D	The model shows each of three units divided into eighths, resulting in a total of 24 units. That is shown as $3 \div \frac{1}{8} = 24$. Although option C is a true statement, it does not represent the model

| 4 | | |

Statements	True	False
$\frac{1}{12} \div 4 > 40$		✓
$\frac{1}{4} \div 7 = \frac{1}{14}$		✓
$\frac{1}{3} \div 33 < 5$	✓	
$\frac{1}{8} \div 4 < \frac{1}{2}$	✓	

1) $\frac{1}{12} \div \frac{4}{1} = \frac{1}{12} \times \frac{1}{4} = \frac{1}{48}$; Therefore $\frac{1}{48} < 40$.

2) $\frac{1}{4} \div 7 = \frac{1}{4} \div \frac{7}{1} = \frac{1}{4} \times \frac{1}{7} = \frac{1}{28}$; Therefore $\frac{1}{28} \neq \frac{1}{14}$

3) $\frac{1}{3} \div 33 = \frac{1}{3} \div \frac{33}{1} = \frac{1}{3} \times \frac{1}{33} = \frac{1}{99}$; Therefore $\frac{1}{99} < 5$

4) $\frac{1}{8} \div 4 = \frac{1}{8} \div \frac{4}{1} = \frac{1}{8} \times \frac{1}{4} = \frac{1}{32}$; Therefore $\frac{1}{32} < \frac{1}{2}$

| 5 | D | As a reader or a writer, you will often need to use more than one text or source at a time. It is important to be able to make comparisons and connections between these sources. |

Question No.	Answer	Detailed Explanation
6	D	Sometimes there is a need to read different texts about a subject. This adds to knowledge about the subject. When several different pieces of information about the same subject are combined, and connections are made, it can broaden one's understanding about the topic.
7 Part A	C	The first sentence in the last paragraph of "Lost in the Woods" reads that the girls are thankful for SAR dogs. There isn't any evidence in the passage to support Choices A, B, or D
7 PArt B	A	"SAR Dogs" tells readers how dogs' sense of smell helps them to find people. In the story "Lost in the Woods," two girls were lost and the dogs found them. After reading "SAR Dogs," readers can figure out how the dog was able to locate the two lost girls (with its sense of smell).
8	B	"SAR Dogs" is told from an objective point of view. Information about the topic was presented without including any of the author's opinions or emotions about the subject.

Question No.	Answer	Detailed Explanation
1	B	In option B, each of 3 units is divided into fourths, resulting in a total of 12 units. Option D also produces 12 units, but it shows 4 units divided into thirds.
2	A	The model shows each of 4 units divided into eighths, resulting in a total of 32 units. That shows how many 1/8 units there are in the 4 whole units.
3	D	Divide $\frac{1}{4}$ mile by 3 to solve: $$\frac{1}{4} \div 3 =$$ $$\frac{1}{4} \times \frac{1}{3} = \frac{1}{12}$$
4	$5\frac{1}{4}$	To determine the maximum length, divide 6 by $1\frac{1}{7}$. $$6 \div 1\frac{1}{7} = 6 \div \frac{8}{7} = \frac{6}{1} \times \frac{7}{8} = \frac{42}{8} = 5\frac{2}{8} = 5\frac{1}{4}$$ Maximum length of the garden is $5\frac{1}{4}$ yards.
5	A	Prepositions are words that introduce and connect. A prepositional phrase begins with a preposition and ends with a noun or pronoun. Verbs show action. Punctuation marks are used to end a sentence.
6	C	The preposition "at" introduces the prepositional phrase "at the loud concert." We is a pronoun, met is a verb, and concert is a noun.
7	B	The object of a preposition is the noun or pronoun that follows the preposition. Generally, any word/words that are between the preposition and object of the preposition are adjectives
8	A	Choice A is the best choice. Tomorrow will be the third day we have lived in the new house. If you read the sentence with each of the other choices, it doesn't sound like it's in the proper form.

Question No.	Answer	Detailed Explanation
1	B	An inch is a larger unit of measure than a centimeter, so the correct answer must be more than one. There are actually 2.54 centimeters to an inch.
2	B	The prefix deci means ten. One dm (decimeter) is 10 centimeters in length.
3	D	There are 12 inches in a foot and 3 feet in a yard. Therefore, each yard is made up of 36 inches ($3 \times 12 = 36$). Seven yards would be 7×36 inches, which is 252.
4	50,000 cm	If 1 meter is 100 centimeters then there are 100 centimeters in one meter. So if the track is 500 meters long it is $500 \times 100 = 50,000$ centimeters long.
5	A	The singular subject Mrs. Smith, takes the singular present tense verb, teaches. This year indicates present tense. Taught is past tense. Teached is an incorrect form. Using teaching in the position of the sentence would require a singular present tense helping verb such as "is."
6	D	Choice A requires the past tense "had." Choice B requires the helping verb "will" along with "have" to agree with the future tense. Choice C requires the third person present tense "has."
7	C	Maggie went rock climbing at the gym yesterday. Choices A and B require the past tense (climbed), and Choice D requires climb
8	Begin	Fruits begin to appear on the orange trees when they are three years old. Began is past tense. Beginning is the progressive or continuous tense in which a helping verb is required.

Question No.	Answer	Detailed Explanation
1	D	The length of each mealworm is shown along the bottom of the line plot. The highest value on the scale is $1\frac{1}{2}$ inches and the Xs above show that there were mealworms this long.
2	A	The length of each mealworm is shown along the bottom of the line plot. The highest value on the scale is $1\frac{1}{2}$ inches and the Xs above show that there were mealworms this long.
3	D	The Xs on the line plot represent the number of mealworms at each length. Since 1 inch has the most Xs above it (4), it is the most common length.
4	D	Number line between 0 and 1 is divided into 8 equal segments. Therefore, the markings refer to $\frac{1}{8}$, $\frac{2}{8}$ etc. First two dots represent two tiles of lengths $\frac{3}{8}$ of an inch. Next three dots represent three tiles of lengths $\frac{4}{8}$ of an inch (Though $\frac{4}{8} = \frac{1}{2}$, it is better to keep the first fraction with denominator 8; it will be easier to add the fractions). Next two tiles have lengths of $\frac{6}{8}$ of an inch and the last one has a length of $\frac{7}{8}$ of an inch. Therefore, total length of the line of tiles (L) is given by, $$L = (2 \times \frac{3}{8}) + (3 \times \frac{4}{8}) + (2 \times \frac{6}{8}) + (1 \times \frac{7}{8})$$ $$L = \frac{6}{8} + \frac{12}{8} + \frac{12}{8} + \frac{7}{8} = \frac{(6+12+12+7)}{8} = \frac{37}{8} = 4\frac{5}{8} \text{ inches}$$ Therefore the correct answer is D.
5	C	The phrase "was playing" is in a singular present tense form. The word were (plural-past) are (plural), and will (future) are incorrect in number and tense. Remember that the number of the subject (whether it is singular or plural) determines the verb because a singular subject must have a singular verb and a plural subject must have a plural verb.
6	B	The verb "are" is plural and requires a plural subject. She and he are all singular subjects and would not agree with a plural verb
7	"can perfect"	In the complete verb phrase "can (never) perfect," never is an adverb, (a negative) and is not part of the complete phrase. Only the helping and main verb are correct.
8	Present	All of the verbs consistently use "present" tense. The verbs are grow, make, jump, and find.

Question No.	Answer	Detailed Explanation
1	D	To find the volume of a rectangular solid, multiply the area of the base (l x w) by the height (h). Therefore, the units are cubic units of length, such as cubic inches.
2	C	To find the volume of a rectangular solid, multiply the area of the base (l x w) by the height (h). In this problem, 4 x 2 x 3 = 24 cubic feet. Therefore, it will take 24 cubes to fill the crate, since each cube is one cubic foot.
3	A	Volume is a measurement of the space an object occupies. It is measured in cubic units.
4	1,1,1	<table><tr><td>Unit cube length</td><td>1</td></tr><tr><td>Unit cube width</td><td>1</td></tr><tr><td>Unit cube height</td><td>1</td></tr></table> Because Oscar wants to determine the volume in cubic inches he should use a cube that represents a cubic inch. Such a cube would be 1 inch by 1 inch by 1 inch.
5	A	Adjectives modify nouns and pronouns. Nouns name persons, places, things, and ideas. Adverbs tell when, where, how, and to what extent. Verbs may be an action or linking and tell what the subject is or does..
6	B	Adverbs are used to modify or describe verbs or even other adverbs. Verbs may be an action or describe the state of being. Adjectives modify nouns. Nouns names persons, places, things, or ideas.
7	A	The most delicious chocolate chip cookies, and the most famous bakery are the correct answers. Because delicious and famous are two syllable words, you should not add er or est to either of them
8	Adverb	The word here as it's used in the above sentence is an adverb. It tells where Robin works.

Day 1

Question No.	Answer	Detailed Explanation
1	D	The volume of a container is measured in cubic units (or units³).
2	D	An object's volume can be determined by packing it with unit cubes, leaving no gaps or overlaps, and counting the number of unit cubes.
3	A	This is the best option because not only is the value reasonable (a cereal box could measure 3 in x 10 in x 12 in, for example), but it also uses units appropriate for measuring volume.
4	B	Count the number of cubes. The picture with 12 cubes has a volume of 12 cubic units. The first picture has 16 cubes, the second 12, the third 8 and the fourth 16.
5	C	Danielle wants neither pizza nor pasta for lunch, because she doesn't like Italian food. Pizza and pasta are both types of Italian food, so since Danielle doesn't like Italian food, she doesn't want it. That makes Choice A incorrect. Choices B and D don't make sense.
6	B	I can't decide whether I should take Spanish class next year or German class. If you're deciding between two options, use the correlating conjunction pair "whether" and "or.
7	B	Neither my mom nor my dad can take me to the library. When you are saying that two options are negative, use the correlative conjunctions "neither" and "nor."
8	D	All of the choices are pairs of correlative conjunctions. Correlative conjunctions are pairs of conjunctions that work together. A writer must use the context of a sentence to choose the appropriate pair of correlative conjunctions to use

Question No.	Answer	Detailed Explanation
1	C	The figure clearly has 15 cubes in the top layer, so there must be another 15 cubes in the bottom layer (the figure is only 2 units high, or 2 layers). Therefore, it has a volume of 30 cubic units (15 + 15 = 30).
2	A	By counting the number of cubes in the figure, you can find that the volume is 30 units^3. There are 3 layers of 8 cubes each in the front part of the figure (3 x 8 = 24) and 3 layers of 2 cubes each at the back of the figure (3 x 2 = 6). Therefore, 24 + 6 = 30.
3	D	By counting the number of cubes in the figure, you can find that the volume is 24 units^3. The bottom layer is 4 by 3 units, so it has a volume of 12 units^3. Each of the top 2 layers is 2 by 3 units, so they each have a volume of 6 units^3. Therefore, 12 + 6 + 6 = 24 units^3.
4		Garrett's building must have exactly 11 cubes. Count the cubes in each design. If the design has 11 cubes answer yes. If not answer is no. First and fourth design have 12 cubes, Second one has 11 cubes, third one has 13 cubes.

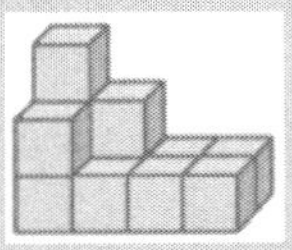

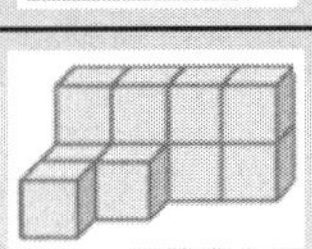

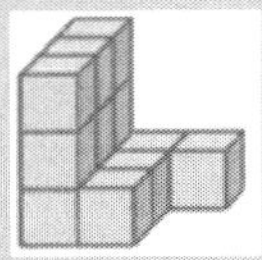

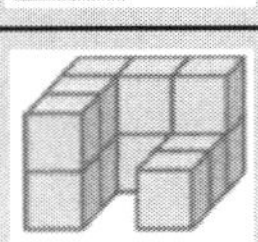

Question No.	Answer	Detailed Explanation
5	B	My cat, Katie, is black and white. Remember that the first word of a sentence must be capitalized. Cat should not be capitalized because it is a common noun; however, Katie is the name of the cat so it needs to be capitalized. You do not capitalize the verb 'is'; adjectives 'black', 'white'; or the conjunction 'and'.
6	C	Nana has two dogs, named Hank and Sugar, who love the back porch. Nana should be capitalized because it's the first word of a sentence and it's a proper noun. Hank and Sugar are the names of dogs, so they should be capitalized. However, back porch and dogs should not be capitalized because they are common nouns.
7	A	"You just missed the bus!" Marrah's mother yelled. "Why can't you ever be on time?" In this sentence, the first word of each of the two sentences should be capitalized (You and Why). Marrah should be capitalized because it is a proper noun and names a specific person. However, mother, a common noun, should not be capitalized.
8	C	Choice C is correct. Capitalize the first word of the beginning of each of the speaker's direct words. Marrah should be capitalized. However, mother should not be capitalized because it is preceded by the word my.

Question No.	Answer	Detailed Explanation
1	D	To find the volume of a rectangular prism, multiply the length x width x height (5 x 5 x 8 = 200).
2	C	To find the volume of a rectangular prism, multiply the length x width x height (6 x 3 x 4 = 72).
3	A	Since the volume (66 ft^3) must equal length x width x height, then 2 x 3 x 11 = 66.
4	24	The volume of the box is equal to the number of cubes that will fit in the box. If six cubes fit on the bottom and there were four layers, the number of cubes is 6 X 4 = 24. Since each cube was 1 foot on each side or volume = 1 cubic feet, the volume of the box is 24 cubic feet.
5	C	"Will your mom take us to school, or do we have to take the bus?" You must capitalize the first word of the sentence. However, you do not capitalize mom in this sentence. You should capitalize mom if it's the first word of the sentence or if you just use the word mom without a pronoun.
6	B	The first word of the sentence should be capitalized. It is a statement so it needs a period at the end. Since "After I scraped the gum off my shoes" begins the sentence, it requires a comma to separate it from the independent clause that follows. It is a subordinate or dependent clause which cannot stand alone. However, if the same phrase were put at the end of the sentence like this, "I went into the house after I scraped the gum off my shoes," then, it doesn't need a comma.
7	A	The first word is capitalized. There are no proper nouns, and the sentence should end with a period because it's a statement. The other choices have the incorrect use of a comma.
8	D	The comma and the conjunction "and" are used to separate the two sentences. Without the conjunction, the sentence would be a run-on.

Week 6

Question No.	Answer	Detailed Explanation
1	B	A box that holds 54 one feet cubes has a volume of 54 ft³. To find the box with this volume, multiply the length x width x height (3 x 2 x 9 = 54).
2	A	The number of 1 inch cubes it can hold is equal to its volume in inches³. To find the volume of the container, multiply the area of the base (30) by its height (5). 30 x 5 = 150.
3	C	The volume of the container (300 cm³) is equal to the area of the base (25) times its height. Therefore, 300 = 25 x 12.
4	B	To find the height of the building, use the formula, Volume(V)=Area of the (B) x height(h) $V = Bh$ $1520 = 95h$ $h = \dfrac{1520}{95} = 16$ feet
5	A	An introductory phrase comes at the beginning of a sentence. It is not the main part of a sentence, but it often gives important information about the sentence. Use a comma to separate the introductory phrase from the rest of the sentence.
6	D	"After the class returned from the playground" is an introductory phrase. Use a comma to separate the introductory phrase from the rest of the sentence.
7	B	"If you always eat breakfast" is an introductory phrase. Use a comma to separate the introductory phrase from the rest of the sentence.
8	C	"Until the whole class gets quiet" is an introductory phrase. Use a comma to separate the introductory phrase from the rest of the sentence.

Question No.	Answer	Detailed Explanation
1	A	To find the total volume, add the volume of the refrigerator (2 x 3 x 4 = 24) to the volume of the freezer (2 x 3 x 2 = 12). 24 + 12 = 36
2	B	To find the volume of one cooler, multiply the length x width x height (30 x 10 x 15 = 4,500). Since Matthew has two coolers, add the two identical volumes: 4,500 + 4,500 = 9,000
3	D	To find the total volume (the number of cubes she can pack), add the volume of the first crate (4 x 4 x 4 = 64) to the volume of the second crate (18 x 2 x 1 = 36). 64 + 36 = 100
4		(see table and explanation below)

Volume of first section in cubic feet	**8284**
Length of the second section in feet	**23**
Volume of the third section in cubic feet	**7512**

(1) Volume of first section = Area of the base x height = 436 x 19 = 8284 cubic feet.

(2) To calculate the lenght of second section, first we have to calculate its volume.

Volume of the second section = Total volume of first and second section - volume of first section = 17254 - 8284 = 8970 cubic feet.

Volume = length x depth x height. Therefore, length = volume / (depth x height) = $\frac{8970}{26 \times 15}$ = $\frac{8970}{390}$ = 23 feet.

(3) Volume of third section = Total volume of the warehouse - (sum of volume of first and second section) = 24766 - 17254 = 7512 cubic feet.

Question No.	Answer	Detailed Explanation
5	A	Sammy, may I go with you to the mall? Use a comma to set off a person's name when you are speaking directly to that person.
6	C	If I could play the guitar like you, Wally, I would join a band. Use a comma to set off a person's name when you are speaking directly to that person.
7	A	Yes, I can help you edit your English essay. Use a comma to set off "yes" and "no" from the rest of the sentence.
8	B	Beau, can I come over and play video games with you? Use a comma to set off a direct address (a person's name such as Beau) from the rest of the sentence.

Question No.	Answer	Detailed Explanation
1	C	A rectangle must have two pairs of parallel sides, so point D must be at 2 on the x-axis (in line with point A) and at 0 on the y-axis (in line with point C).
2	B	Segment AB (from 2 to 5) is 3 units long. Segment BC (from 0 to 4) is 4 units long. Segment BC is longer.
3	B	Using the labels, follow the x-axis as far as point R (7 units) and the y-axis as far as point R (2 units). This makes the coordinate pair (7, 2).
4	C	The x-axis is the horizontal line in a coordinate grid and is represented by the letter T in the picture.
5	B	Choice B is the correct answer. You should use quotation marks to emphasize titles of poems, short stories, songs, and other short written works.
6	B	Choice B is correct. You should use quotation marks to emphasize titles of poems, short stories, songs, and other short written works.
7	B	Choice B is correct. You should use quotation marks to emphasize titles of poems, short stories, songs, and other short written works
8	D	Choice D is correct. You can use underlining (Choice C) or italics (Choice A) to indicate titles of plays, books, newspapers, magazines, movies, and other complete works. Typically, these titles are underlined when they are handwritten and in italics when they are typed.

Question No.	Answer	Detailed Explanation
1	C	The location of the weather station is at the intersection of 9 on the x-axis and 2 on the y-axis. Therefore, its coordinates are (9,2).
2	B	The location of the warehouse is at the intersection of 0 on the x-axis and 4 on the y-axis. Therefore, its coordinates are (0,4).
3	A	At the intersection of 7 on the x-axis and 2 on the y-axis, the hospital is located.

4

	True	False
Lui reach mile marker 1.0 in seven minutes. The x-coordinate associated the y = 1.0 is 7.	●	
It took Lui two minutes to run from mile marker 1.0 to mile marker 1.2. Lui was at mile marker 1.0 at 7 minutes. She reached mile marker 1.2 at 12 minutes. Thus it took her 12-7 = 5 minutes to run from mile marker 1.0 to 1.2.		●
Lui ran from mile marker 1.1 to mail marker 1.2 in three minutes. Lui was at mile marker 1.1 at 10 minutes. She reached mile marker 1.2 at 12 minutes. Thus it took her 12-10 = 2 minutes to run from mile marker 1.1 to 1.2.		●
Fourteen minutes after Lui started she reached mile marker 1.3. The y-coordinate associated with x = 14 is 1.3.	●	

Question No.	Answer	Detailed Explanation
5	D	The correct spelling is incredible. The prefix is in-, the root word is cred, and the suffix is -ible. There are many words that end with this suffix.
6	B	The correct spelling should be usually. Be aware of the word weather because it is often confused with whether.
7	seamed	The correct spelling for the past tense of the linking verb seem is seemed.
8	Impatience	The correct spelling is impatience. Impatience is a noun, but impatient is an adjective.

Question No.	Answer	Detailed Explanation
1	C	In a regular plane figure, all sides are equal lengths and all angles are congruent. However the angles do not have to total 180.
2	D	Similar shapes do not have to be the same size, but they must be the same shape. All sides must have the same ratio. Since circles, squares, and equilateral triangles always have the same ratio of sides (or dimension, in the case of the circle), they are always similar.
3	C	Remember that the three interior angles of a triangle always equal 180 degrees. If two of the angles equal 80 degrees, the third angle must be 100 degrees. Any triangle with an angle greater than 90 degrees is obtuse.

4

	True	False
All squares are rhombuses.	●	
All parallelograms have four right angles.		●
All trapezoids have at least one set of parallel sides.	●	
All squares are rectangles.	●	

(1) Since all sides of a square are equal, a square is also a rhombus. Therefore, 1st statement is true.

(2) All parallelograms need not have four right angles. Therefore, 2nd statement is false.

(3) A trapezoid has only one pair of parallel lines. Therefore, 3rd statement is true.

(4) Each angle of a square measure 90 degrees. So, every square is also a rectangle. Therefore, 4th statement is true.

Question No.	Answer	Detailed Explanation
5	C	Choice C is correct. An independent clause is a group of words that has a subject and a verb, expresses a complete thought, and can stand alone. A dependent clause has a subject and a verb, but it does not express a complete thought and cannot stand alone. It must be attached to an independent clause. We call this a complex sentence when you have an independent and a dependent clause joined together. A coordinating conjunction is just one of the parts of speech that is used to join words, phrases, or sentence
6	C	A group of words that has a subject and a verb, does not express a complete thought, and cannot stand alone is called a dependent clause. Remember that an independent clause doesn't need a dependent clause, but a dependent clause needs an independent clause. It's just like an independent person who can take care of himself or herself, but a dependent person requires the aid and support of someone else who should be and is most likely independent..
7	C	"When Juan studied for his quiz at the library" is not a complete sentence or an independent clause. Although it has a subject (Juan) and a verb (studied), it does not express a complete thought and cannot stand on its own. The subordinating conjunction "when" makes the sentence dependent. Without the first word, "when", the group of words would be an independent clause. Remember that subordinating conjunctions turn independent clauses into dependent clauses.
8	B	Miguel loves cars, but he can never find the time to work on one. This is an example of a compound sentence that is joined together by the comma and a coordinating conjunction. Both sentences have a subject and a verb (Miguel loves... and he can (never) find). Both sentences can stand alone, because they express a complete thought. You could make this a complex sentence by adding a subordinating conjunction to the beginning of the sentence which would turn the independent clause into a dependent clause (Although Miguel loves cars). Although Miguel loves cars, he can never find the time to work on one. This is a complex sentence, because it is composed of a dependent clause and an independent clause.

Question No.	Answer	Detailed Explanation
1	C	A square is both a rhombus and a rectangle.
2	A	Scalene is a type of triangle that is not isosceles.
3	B	An isosceles triangle can also be a right triangle (one with a 90° angle). Then it is called an isosceles right triangle.
4	B	A rhombus and a square are both parallelograms with four equal sides. The square, however, has equal angles (90 degrees each). Therefore the correct answer is 'B' the rhombus.
5	B	Choice A is incorrect, because Francine wouldn't bother to introduce herself to a stranger if she was arrogant. Choice C is incorrect, because Francine shows that she's not serious by comparing Adam to a cold glass of lemonade. Choice D is incorrect, because Francine seems excited which is the opposite of bored.
6	C	Adam can be described as proper due to the way he formally introduces himself to Francine. Choices A and D are incorrect, because casual and silly are nearly opposites of proper. Choice B is incorrect, because William would have ignored Francine if she was rude.
7	C	Francine is likely from the southern part of the United States. Because she compared meeting Adam to a cold glass of water on a hot summer day, it seems she is from the South. Southern people often use expressions such as this one and are known for their friendliness
8	C	"I reckon" means "I think." This is an example of a dialect and it is often used in the southern region of the United States.

Question No.	Answer	Detailed Explanation
1	B	The Associative Property of Multiplication states that when three or more numbers are multiplied, the product will be the same no matter how the three numbers are grouped. In this example, multiplying 11 x 6 x 7 will produce the same result whether the 11 x 6 are grouped together in parentheses or the 6 x 7 are grouped together. The other options are all mathematically correct, but they show different properties of multiplication
2	A	When working with parentheses ( ) and brackets [ ], work from the inside to the outside. $[(3 \times 2) + 4] \div 5 \rightarrow [6 + 4] \div 5 \rightarrow 10 \div 5 \rightarrow 2$ $2 \times [(5 \times 4) \div 10] \rightarrow 2 \times [20 \div 10] \rightarrow 2 \times 2 \rightarrow 4$ $12 - [(4 + 8) \div 3] \rightarrow 12 - [12 \div 3] \rightarrow 12 - 4 \rightarrow 8$
3		Think twenty divided by what is ten. Twenty divided by 2 is 10. Therefore two must equal what is in the brackets, $2=[5-(a ? 9)]$. Next think, five minus what is two. Five minus three is two. Therefore three must equal what is in the parentheses, $3=(a ? 9)$. Now, we can get 3 by subtracting 9 from 12. $3=12-9$. We can also divide 27 by 9 to get 3. $3 = 27 \div 9$
4	B	$6 \times 8 = 48$ $6 \times 10 = 60$ $48 + 60 = 108.$ Hence, answer choice B is correct.
5	B	A clue to this meaning is that my mother chased it with a broom.
6	D	If you insert the word chewed in place of gnawed, the meaning is still workable.
7	A	Jan ran away in disgust. The fact that she ran indicates that she was frightened of what she saw, so it must have been ugly. It's not typical to run away from something that is beautiful.
8	D	Direct context clues explicitly define a word in a sentence. There are no unusual clues, and it's not necessary to infer or read between the lines. The meaning is directly stated.

Question No.	Answer	Detailed Explanation
1	B	First, subtract the 9 that Olivia kept for herself (42 – 9). Then divide the difference among the three friends: (42 – 9) ÷ 3.
2	C	The expression 8 x (467 + 509) indicates that you should first find the sum of 467 and 509, and then multiply by 8. Therefore, the solution is 8 times greater than that sum.
3	A	The expression (3,259 – 741) ÷ 3 indicates that you should first find the difference of 3,259 and 741, and then divide by 3. Therefore, the solution is one third as much as that difference.
4	B	First, multiply 7 items by the 25 students (25 x 7). Then add to that product the 13 the teacher sold: 13 + (25 x 7).
5	D	Suffixes are added to the end of a word, such as the word quickly. The suffix is -ly. A prefix is added to the beginning of a word, such as restate. Re- is a prefix. An affix means that something can be attached to a word and it changes the meaning.
6	C	The word unhappy has a prefix of un, which means "not." Unhappy literally means not happy. So, if you are unhappy about something, it means you are the opposite of happy (sad).
7	C	The prefix bi-, added to cycle forms the word bicycle, meaning two wheels. The prefix tri, means three, and quad means four. The word dual means having two like parts or a double.
8	Comfort	The word comfort, is the root word in the word uncomfortable. Uncomfortable has a prefix and a suffix. The word means not able to be comfortable

Day 2

Question No.	Answer	Detailed Explanation
1	B	The rule is divide by 3, then add 2, so plugging in each input number results in the following: $9 \div 3 + 2 = 5$, $15 \div 3 + 2 = 7$, $27 \div 3 + 2 = 11$, $33 \div 3 + 2 = 13$. To create coordinate pairs, write the input number followed by the output number, separated by a comma, in parentheses.
2	D	The rule is -4, Option (A) is incorrect. because $0 - 4 = -4$ and not 1. (If the rule does not work for one number, we need not check for other numbers). Option (B) is incorrect, because $3 - 4 = -1$ and not 1. Option (C) is incorrect, because $4 - 4 = 0$ and not 1. All the numbers in option (D) satisfies the rule. $5 - 4 = 1$, $11 - 4 = 7$, $14 - 4 = 10$, $19 - 4 = 15$
3	D	The rule is +1, x5, Option (A) is incorrect. because $(2 + 1) \times 5 = 15$ not 5. (If the rule does not work for one number, we need not check for other numbers). Option (B) is incorrect, because $(1 + 1) \times 5 = 10$ not 5 Option (C) is incorrect, because $(30 + 1) \times 5 = 155$ not 5 All the numbers in option (D) satisfies the rule. $(0 + 1) \times 5 = 5$, $(3 + 1) \times 5 = 20$, $(6 + 1) \times 5 = 35$, $(10 + 1) \times 5 = 55$.
4	D	If the value of x increases while the value of y decreases, the function produces a downward sloping straight line.
5	C	When you look up a word in a dictionary, you will see its pronunciation. That means that you will get a phonetic spelling of the word so that you will know how to say it.
6	D	A dictionary provides meanings of unknown words. Choice A is incorrect, because another mystery book would not provide a definition. Choice B is incorrect, because mystery books do not usually contain glossaries. Choice C is incorrect, because a thesaurus provides a list of synonyms.
7	D	A thesaurus is a reference book that has synonyms. Use a thesaurus to find different, interesting words when you are writing.
8	All of the above	All of the following information can be found in a dictionary: correct spellings, definitions, parts of speech (verb, noun, adjective, etc.), and also word origins.

Question No.	Answer	Detailed Explanation
1	C	Write the number 4 in the ones place. The word 'and' indicates the decimal point. The fractional part of the number is three-hundredths, which is shown with a 3 in the hundredths place. Use a placeholder 0 in the tenths place, so the 3 is two places to the right of the decimal.
2	A	The 6 is seven places to the left of the decimal, which is the millions place. Its value is 6 million.
3	C	The 9 is three places to the right of the decimal, which is the thousandths place. Its value is 9 thousandths.
4	D	In order for two numbers to be equal, they must have the same digits in the same place value. In this option, each number has a 5 in the tenths place. The final zeros after the tenths place do not change the value
5	B	The boys ran off like rockets shooting up to the stars means that the boys ran away quickly. Rockets shooting up to the stars would have to be extremely fast. The boys running away were extremely fast. A simile compares two unlike objects using like or as.
6	A	Dad's business runs like a well-oiled machine means that the business is run or managed very smoothly. That means everyone knows what they're supposed to do, and there are rarely any difficulties. A metaphor is a direct comparison of two unlike objects
7	B	My best friend and I are like two peas in a pod means that the two friends are very similar. They might look alike, act alike, and like similar things. This is a simile, because it compares two unlike things using like or as.
8	D	Without my glasses, I'm as blind as a bat means that the person can't see very well without eyeglasses. Bats live in the dark, and without glasses the person can't see very well, it's like they're in the dark.

Week 8

Question No.	Answer	Detailed Explanation
1	D	10^5 means 10 x 10 x 10 x 10 x 10, which equals 100,000. 3 x 100,000 = 300,000. Another way to think of this problem is 3 x 10 = 30, then make sure the number of zeros in the answer matches the number of the exponent (5), which is 300,000.
2	C	10^4 means 10 x 10 x 10 x 10, which equals 10,000. 6.9 ÷ 10,000 = 0.00069. Another way to think of this problem is to move the decimal in 6.9 to the left (because it is division) the number of places equal to the exponent (4).
3	B	The decimal point is being moved to the left, so it is a division problem. Since it is being moved 7 places, 8.2 is being divided by 10^7.
4	C	Since the decimal point in 477.0 is being moved five places to the right, it is being multiplied by 100,000. This number can be shown as 10^5.
5	C	A proverb is a phrase which contains advice or a generally accepted truth. An example of a proverb is "look before you leap."
6	C	"Do not put all your eggs in one basket" has a similar meaning to "do not store all of your data on one computer." It means that you shouldn't keep important data in one place, because something destructive might happen where it's stored.
7	B	Alliteration is the repetition of a particular sound in a series of words like tongue twisters. A proverb and an adage can be confused, but proverbs tend to give advice or wisdom, whereas an adage is a short memorable phrase that is passed around and becomes accepted as a truth.
8	Keep it Secret	Keep it a secret, is what the idiom "don't let the cat out of the bag," means. It is not a literal meaning to keep a real cat in a bag

Day 5

Question No.	Answer	Detailed Explanation
1	B	In the number 0.05, the 5 is in the hundredths place. To show this amount (five hundredths) as a fraction, use 5 as the numerator and 100 as the denominator.
2	D	One half is equal to five tenths (think of a pizza sliced into 10 pieces, half of the pizza would be 5 out of 10 slices). To show five tenths, use a 5 in the tenths place immediately to the right of the decimal.
3	A	Sixty hundredths is equivalent to six tenths (the place to the right of the decimal). Three hundredths is shown by a 3 in the hundredths place (two places to the right of the decimal).
4	D	In expanded form, each digit is multiplied by its place value and the products are added together. The expression $9 \times 10 + 2 \times 1 + 3 \times (\frac{1}{10}) + 8 \times (\frac{1}{100})$ can be thought of as: $9 \times 10 = 90$ $2 \times 1 = 2$ $3 \times (\frac{1}{10}) = .3$ $8 \times (\frac{1}{100}) = .08$ Add the products to get 92.38
5	A	Antonyms are words that are opposite in meaning. Roar, growl, and loud are similar in meaning, but opposite to the meaning of the word murmur, which means a very low sound that's barely audible.
6	A	Synonyms are words that have similar meanings.
7	D	Antonyms are words that have opposite meanings. A way to remember the difference between antonym and synonym is to recall the letter "a" (antonym) and link it with the word against (opposite), and recall the letter "s" (synonym) and link it with the word same or similar
8	D	highest and lowest, are antonyms or opposite in meaning. They are also at the very opposite ends of a spectrum or range of scores.

Week 9

Question No.	Answer	Detailed Explanation
1	D	Each of these options involves comparing decimals (since the numbers to the left of the decimal point in each option are equal). Remember, the further a number is to the right of a decimal, the lower its place value. Be sure to compare numbers that are in the same place value (compare tenths to tenths, etc.). For each of these options, compare the underlined digit: 48.01 = 48.1 These are not equal, because .0 is less than .1. 25.4_ < 25.40 The final zero does not affect the number's value, so these two numbers are equal. 10.83 < 10.093 The 8 in the tenths place is greater than a 0 in the tenths place. 392.01 < 392.1 This is correct because .1 is greater than .0.
2	C	In order to compare the size of numbers, begin with the place value furthest to the left. In this case, three of the numbers have a 1 in the ones place, so look to the tenths place to compare those three. The number with the lowest digit in the tenths place will come first (1.02) followed by the number with the next-highest digit in the tenths place (1.12) followed by the number with the highest digit in the tenths place (1.2). The remaining number has a 2 in the ones place, so it is the greatest.
3	C	Each of these options involves comparing similar digits in different place values. Be sure to compare numbers that are in the same place value (compare tenths to tenths, etc.), starting with the highest place value. For each of these options, compare the underlined digit: _3.21 > 32.1 No tens is less than 3 tens. _32.12 > 312.12 No hundreds is less than 3 hundreds. 32.12 > 3.212 This is correct because 3 tens is more than no tens. 212.3 < 21.32 Two hundreds is greater than no hundreds.
4	A	The missing number must be greater than 4.17 but less than 4.19. Since the ones place (4) and tenths place (1) are the same, the missing number will begin with 4.1 as well. Looking to the hundredths place, the missing number must fall between 7 and 9. That makes it 4.18.
5	C	The word obsolete means no longer produced or used. Video tapes are nearly obsolete, because movies are more commonly sold in DVD format now.

Question No.	Answer	Detailed Explanation
6	A	The word provide means to make available for use. When you provide someone your phone number, it means you are giving it to them so that they can use it to call you.
7	B	Retain means to hold onto or keep. One may retain a receipt which means to keep it, in case the item needs to be returned in the future.
8	D	The people of the village were tired of being treated badly, so they decided to overthrow the king. Overthrow means to remove from leadership.

Question No.	Answer	Detailed Explanation
1	D	In order for a number to round to 13.75, it must be between 13.745 and 13.754. The number 13.747 has a 7 in the thousandths place that means it will round up to 13.75.
2	B	Round $5.91 up to $6. Round $7.27 down to $7. Round $12.60 up to $13. $6 + $7 + $13 = $26.
3	C	Round 6.21 up to 7 and 2.5 up to 3. She needs two 7 feet pieces (=14 feet) and one 3 feet piece. She will have to buy about 17 feet (14 + 3) of wood.
4	C	The answer options indicate that this problem can be solved using estimation. Round 13.2 down to 13 and 62 down to 60. 13 x 60 = 780, which is closest to the option '800 points.'
5	C	There isn't any evidence in the passage that indicates that there was a storm that crashed the cupboard when the king was gone. The statement that people in the passage accidentally broke the glass cupboard is not accurate. However, it does say that the thieves broke into the palace and stole the glass cupboard. "None of the above" does not apply.
6	A	There is evidence in the passage that correctly supports the answer that the thieves took gold out of the cupboard. However, there isn't evidence that there were silver, diamonds, or stones taken from the cupboard, so these answer choices are incorrect..
7	D	There isn't evidence in the passage to support that the thieves were told to take everything out of the cupboard, to break the cupboard, or to take gold out of the cupboard. However, there is evidence to support that the thieves should have remembered to put something back into the cupboard each time that they took something out.
8 Part A	D	There is evidence in the passage to support the correct answer that Sam ran after the traveler to get one of his chickens. However, there is no evidence to support that Sam ran after the traveler because he wanted him to stay, or to get one of the traveler's ears or shoes
8 Part B	B	The passage indicates that the traveler picked up his shoes and ran out of the house because he was scared. However, when the traveler went to wash up, the wife was supposed to have chicken cooked and ready for the traveler to eat. The passage indicates that the traveler was weary or tired, but there isn't evidence to support that the traveler was curious. He was frightened into running off. None of the above is incorrect, because there is an answer from the given choices.

Question No.	Answer	Detailed Explanation
1	B	According to the Distributive Property of Multiplication, you can break one of the factors (101) into two parts (100 and 1) and multiply them both by the other factor. 596 x 100 and 596 x 1 will produce the same answer as multiplying 596 x 100 and adding 596 more.
2	C	Three of the trays held 15 cookies each, so 3 x 15 = 45. The other six trays held 18 cookies each, so 6 x 18 = 108. To find the total, add 45 + 108 = 153.
3	A	In the first step, 3 x 8 is recorded as 32. It should be 24.
4		When multiplying multi-digit numbers, multiply one number by each of the place value in the second number and then add the results together. The number 5321 in expanded form is 5000 + 300 + 20 + 1. Therefore the completed table is as follows:

268	×	1	=	268
268	×	**20**	=	5,360
268	×	300	=	80,400
268	×	**5000**	=	**1340000**
268	×	Total	=	**1426028**

Question No.	Answer	Detailed Explanation
5	A	The evidence shows that this passage is about being determined. The narrator did not give up. She listens to friends and takes a deep breath, but these are the details in the story, not the main idea. Remember that the sum of the details is the main idea which is what the story is mostly about.
6	D	Choice D is correct. The evidence in this story that supports that Katie was nervous at the beginning is her blushing and wringing her hands. There is not enough information in the story to support that Katie was depressed. Do not confuse the crowd's excitement to mean that Katie felt the same way. While at the beginning she was nervous, she seems relieved at the end or glad that it was over. Because Katie had so many people happy for her, one might assume that she was friendly, but there isn't any evidence to support that in the story.
7 Part A	A	Choice A is correct. In the passage above, Katie was blushing, wringing her hands, and nervous. This evidence supports that her friends likely thought she would stand there or walk off stage. However, after Katie calmed herself, the passage shows that Katie was able to sing a beautiful song as her friends listened and paid attention to her.

Question No.	Answer	Detailed Explanation
7 Part B	B	Choice B is correct. According to the second paragraph in the passage, there is evidence that Katie is not going to give up and is getting control of her nervousness, but the main thing is to show Katie's strength. She pulls herself together so that she can sing. There is no evidence in the passage to support that Katie is being silly.
8	D	Choice D is correct. The best title for this poem is "No Time," because the author speaks about how being busy can make a person miss out on the simple things in life, like enjoying leisure time and standing and staring. There isn't any evidence to indicate "hard work." Although "stand and stare" is mentioned, it is always referenced to no time

Question No.	Answer	Detailed Explanation
1	D	No number that can be divided by zero.
2	A	100 divided by 12 is 8 with remainder 4 = 8 R 4 $= 8 \frac{4}{12}$

Show Work:

```
        0 0 8
  1 2 | 1 0 0
        0
        1 0
          0
        1 0 0
          9 6
            4
```

After filling 8 boxes, there will be a remainder of 4 donuts.

Question No.	Answer	Detailed Explanation
3	B	Any number divided by 1 remains the same.
4	B	680 divided by 40 is 17 with remainder 0 = 17 R 0 $= 17 \frac{0}{14}$

Show Work:

```
        0 1 7
  4 0 | 6 8 0
        0
        6 8
        4 0
        2 8 0
        2 8 0
            0
```

Question No.	Answer	Detailed Explanation
5	A	The last stanza of this poem states that one who has everything, but doesn't have time to stop and stare (look longingly at something), has a poor life. Another way of looking at this is to ask what good is it to have everything if you can't enjoy it? There isn't any evidence to support that life is good, so the other two statements are incorrect. Remember that if a statement is supported by a comma, both parts of the statement must be correct. If one part is false, the entire statement is false.
6	C	From the given choices, the best title for this poem is "Stop and Stare," because it supports the overall meaning of the story which tells the reader that a full life includes having time to stop and stare or just to rest and look at something for a while. "Life" is too general because the focus is not on life, but taking time to enjoy something in life. "Stare" and "Life and Stare" do not have supporting evidence in the story. The title can give the reader a clue to the message or theme of a piece, and "Stop and Stare" provides that information.
7	A	There is no evidence in this poem to support a message that the family is unpredictable. The last line clearly shows that the author believes that his family will take care of him, so that makes the choice "they are too crazy to care" incorrect. Even though the author describes each family member like different animals, the author is not trying to say that they are animals. Refer to the last line, where the evidence points out that their differences do not keep them from caring for each other.
8	C	This poem uses personification (non-human objects are given human qualities) to describe the various noises in the kitchen. "The Kitchen" is the most appropriate title because it is the setting, which is very important to this passage. Since the poem only briefly mentions, "The Sink," "The Plate," and "The Refrigerator," they are mere details and are not the focus of the poem.

Question No.	Answer	Detailed Explanation
1	C	To solve, use division. Divide the numbers without the decimal point. Then, insert a decimal into the answer, leaving the same number of places to the right of the decimal as the dividend. 42 ÷ 3 = 14 --> 0.14
2	D	To solve, use division. Move both decimal places to the right one place, so you are dividing by a whole number (0.9 ÷ 3). Divide the numbers without the decimal point. Then, insert a decimal into the answer, leaving the same number of places to the right of the decimal as the dividend (remember that you shifted the decimal to have only one place to the right of the dividend). 9 ÷ 3 = 3 --> 0.3
3	C	When adding decimals, line up the decimals and add any necessary zeros to the end of the numbers so they have the same number of decimal places. Then add each place value as normal bringing down the decimal in the same location as in the original numbers. 12.83 45.70 +5.47 64.00
4	10.31	Subtract the numbers, keeping their place values in line. Bring the decimal straight down to the solution. Remember that the number 12.3 can be written as 12.30. 1 12 10 12. 3 0 - 1. 9 9 1 0. 3 1
5	D	After Marrah got her backpack, her mother smiled and said, "Let's go to school, Marrah." Marrah's mother called upstairs to her to come down, and reminded her that she always missed the bus are evidence of her mother's frustration, and she didn't remain in this mood. She smiled and took her to school. Be sure that you read the question carefully and examine each answer choice closely to ensure that it addresses the question. The answer choices that are incorrect are so because they don't address the question asked. However, they may be true for another question if it were asked. But, be very careful not to create your own questions to fit an incorrect answer choice because you may unintentionally select the wrong answer.

Question No.	Answer	Detailed Explanation
6	C	Rosebud is shy and scared, even though she overcomes these traits at the end of the story. There is no evidence in the story to support that Rosebud is colorful, generous, and fearless. In fact, she was very cautious. Because Rosebud lives in the dark underground, there isn't evidence that she expects company, so she is not seen as excited, happy, or friendly right away. In the end, after she had let in Sun and Rain and seen the beautiful garden, she realized that she was the most beautiful flower, which probably made her happy and excited. But, there is no evidence given in the story to support this.
7		Rosebud is shy and scared and lives underground. She is initially very cautious when the sun and rain come knocking. However, she overcomes her fear in the end and emerges out as one of the prettiest pink rose in the whole garden.
8	A	This story is about what can happen when you are disorganized. The character Marrah was very disorganized and was late to school. In some answer choices, like the last one, the statement can be made correct by substituting the opposite word for "disorganized," which is organized. Remember that a detail, like the argument between Marrah and her mother, is not what the story or passage is mainly about. Details add up to the main purpose or idea.

STOP! IN THE NAME OF EDUCATION: PREVENT SUMMER LEARNING LOSS WITH 7 SIMPLE STEPS

Summer Learning loss is defined as "a loss of knowledge and skills . . . most commonly due to . . . . extended breaks [during the summertime] " (from edglossary.org/learning-loss). Many teachers have certainly had the experience of taking the first month of school not only to introduce his or her rules and procedures to the class but also to get the kids back "up to speed" with thinking, remembering what they've learned . . . and in many cases, reviewing previous content. With a traditional school calendar, then, this can mean that up to 10% of the school year is spent playing catch-up.

What's a parent to do? Fortunately, there are some simple steps you can take with your child to help your son or daughter both enjoy the summer and keep those all-important skills honed and fresh:

(1) Read!

Research supports the relationship between independent reading and student achievement, so simply having your child read daily will make a positive difference. Check out the following sources to find books that your child will want to dive into: your public library, local bookstores, online stores (Amazon, Barnes and Noble, half.com, etc.), and yard sales (if the family hosting the sale has children a bit older than your own, you stand a good chance of scoring discarded books that are a perfect match for your son or daughter's reading level).

(2) Write!

Have your child write letters to out-of-town friends and family, or write postcards while on vacation. A summer journal is another way to document summer activities. For the artistic or tech-savvy child, you may choose to create a family scrapbook with captions (consider the online options at Shutterfly, Mixbook, and Smilebox). Not only will you preserve this summer's memories, but your child will also continue to practice his or her writing skills! (See Summer is Here! Ideas to Keep Your Child's Writing Skills Sharp for more writing ideas.)

(3) Do the Math!

Think of ways your child can incorporate math skills into daily activities: have a yard sale, and put your child in charge of the cash box; help younger ones organize a lemonade stand (to practice salesmanship and making change). Or simply purchase a set of inexpensive flash cards to practice basic facts while waiting in line or on a long car ride. There's even a host of free online games that will keep your child's math skills sharp.

(4) "Homeschool" Your Child

Keeping your child's skills fresh doesn't have to cost a fortune: check out some of the Lumos Learning workbooks and online resources (at lumoslearning.com/store), and your child can work through several exercises each day. Even as little as twenty minutes a day can yield positive results, and it's easy to work in a small block of time here and there. For instance, your child can work in the book during a car ride, right before bedtime, etc. Or, simply make this part of your child's morning routine. For example: wake up, eat breakfast, complete chores, and then work in the workbook for 20 minutes. With time, you can make this a natural habit.

(5) Go Back-to-School Shopping (For a Great Summer School Learning Experience)

Check out offerings from the big names (think Sylvan, Huntington, Mathnasium, and Kumon), and also consider local summer schools. Some school districts and local colleges provide learning programs: research the offerings on-line for more information regarding the available options in your area.

(6) Take a Hike . . . Go Camping!

But "camp" doesn't always involve pitching a tent in the great outdoors. Nowadays, there are camps for every interest: sports camps, art camp, music camp, science camp, writing camp . . . the possibilities are endless! With a quick Internet search, you'll be able to turn up multiple options that will appeal to your son or daughter. And even if these camps aren't "academic", the life skills and interpersonal experiences are certain to help your child succeed in the "real world". For example, working together as a cast to put on a summer theater production involves memorizing lines, cooperation, stage crew coordination, and commitment – all skills that can come in handy when it comes to fostering a good work ethic and the ability to collaborate with others.

(7) Get tutored

Many teachers offer tutoring services throughout the summer months, either for individuals or small groups of students. Even the most school-averse student tends to enjoy the personal attention of a former teacher in a setting outside of the classroom. Plus, a tutor can tailor his or her instruction to pinpoint your child's needs – so you can maximize the tutoring sessions with the skills and concepts your child needs the most help with.

Of course, you don't need to do all seven steps to ensure that your child maintains his or her skills. Just following through with one or two of these options will go a long way toward continued learning, skills maintenance, and easing the transition to school when summer draws to a close.

SUMMER READING: QUESTIONS TO ASK THAT PROMOTE COMPREHENSION

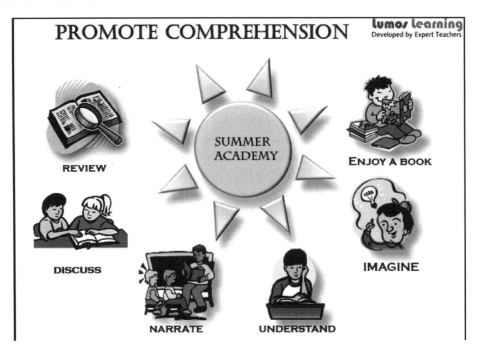

As mentioned in our "Beating Summer Academic Loss" article, students are at risk of losing academic ground during the summer months, especially with respect to their reading level, spelling, and vocabulary. One of the best ways to prevent this "brain drain" for literacy is to have your son or daughter read each day during the summer break.

Better yet, you can promote these all-important skills and participate in your child's summer reading by engaging in active dialogue with your son or daughter. Below are several questions and ideas for discussion that will promote comprehension, recall, and critical thinking skills. In addition, these questions reflect several of the Common Core standards – which underpin the curriculum, instruction and standardized testing for most school districts. Of course, the standards vary by grade level, but some of the common themes that emerge in these standards are: citing evidence, summarizing, and making inferences.

• Citing evidence

Simply put, citing evidence involves going back into the text (book, magazine, newspaper, etc.) and finding "proof" to back up an answer, opinion, or assertion. For instance, you could ask your child, "Did you enjoy this book?" and then follow up that "yes" or "no" response with a "Why?" This requires the reader to provide details and examples from the story to support his or her opinion. For this particular question, then, your child may highlight plot events he or she liked, character attributes, writing style, and even genre (type of book) as evidence. Challenge for older students: Ask your child to go back into the text and find a direct quote to support an opinion or answer.

• Summarizing

For nonfiction pieces, this may involve being able to explain the 5W's – who, what, where, when, why (and how). For literature, ask your child to summarize the story elements, including: the setting, characters, main conflict or problem, events, resolution, and theme/lesson/moral. If your child can do this with specificity and accuracy, there's a very good chance that he or she comprehended the story. Challenge for older students: Ask your child to identify more complex story elements, such as the climax, rising action, and falling action.

• Making inferences

Making an inference is commonly referred to as "reading between the lines." That is, the reader can't find the answer to a question directly in the text but instead must synthesize or analyze information to come to a conclusion. To enhance these higher-level thinking skills, ask your child to describe the main character's personality, describe how a character changed by the end of a novel, or detail how the setting influenced the story's plot. Challenge for older students: Have the reader compare and contrast two or more characters to highlight similarities and differences in personality, actions, etc.

 Of course, if you read the same book that your child reads, you'll be able to come up with even more detailed questions – and also know if your child truly understood the reading based on his or her answers! But even if you don't get a chance to read what your child does, simply asking some of these questions not only helps your child's reading skills but also demonstrates an interest in your child – and his or her reading.

BEATING THE BRAIN DRAIN THROUGH LITERACY: WEBINAR RECAP WITH PRINTABLE ACTIVITY SHEET

Lumos Learning conducted webinar on "Beating the Brain Drain Through Literacy." During this webinar, we provided the students with several ideas for keeping their literacy skills sharp in the summertime.

Here's a handy chart with the ideas from the webinar, ready for you to post on your refrigerator. Let your child pick and choose the activities that appeal to him or her. Of course, reading should be nonnegotiable, but the list below provides alternatives for reluctant readers – or for those who just don't enjoy reading a traditional fiction novel. The first set of activities touch upon ideas that reinforce writing skills, while the second half addresses reading skills. There is also room on the chart to date or check off activities your child has completed.

Skill Area	Activity	Completed this activity	Notes for parents
Writing skills, spelling, and/or vocabulary	Keep a journal (things you do, places you go, people you meet)		Even though journals work on spelling skills, be sure your child understands that spelling "doesn't count". Most children like to keep their journals private, so they don't need to worry about perfect skills or that someone else is going to read/grade what they wrote.
	Start a blog		Enable privacy settings to keep viewers limited to friends and family. Check out WordPress, Squarespace, and Quillpad to begin blogging.
	Get published		The following places publish student work: The Clairmont Review, CyberKids, Creative Kids Magazine, New Moon, and The Young Writer's Magazine.
	Write letters		Have your child write or type letters, postcards, and emails to friends and family members.
	Take part in a family movie night		Watch movies that are thought-provoking to elicit interesting post-movie discussions. Other good bets are movies that are based on a book (read the book first and compare the two).
	Organize a family game night		Choose word games to work on spelling and vocabulary skills (examples: Scrabble, Boggle, and Hangman).
Reading skills: fluency, comprehension, critical thinking, decoding skills,inferencing, etc.	Pick up a good book!		Places to find/buy/borrow books include: your public library, ebooks, yard sales, book stores, your child's school library (if it's open during the summer), and borrowed books from friends and family members.
	Read materials that aren't "books"…		Ideas include: karaoke lyrics, cereal boxes, newspapers, magazines for kids, billboards, close captioning, and audio books.
	Compete! Enter a reading challenge		Scholastic Reading hosts a competition called "Reading Under the Stars" to break a world record for minutes read. Barnes and Noble gives students the opportunity to earn one free book with "Imagination's Destination" reading challenge.

Note: Reading just six books over the summer can maintain – and sometimes even increase! – your child's reading level. Not sure if the book is appropriate for your child's reading level? Use the five-finger rule: have your son/daughter read a page of a book. Each time your child encounters a word that is unfamiliar or unknown, he or she holds up a finger. If your child holds up more than five fingers on a given page, that book is probably too difficult.

However, there are some books that a child will successfully tackle if it's high-interest to him or her. Keep in mind that reading levels are a guide (as is the five-finger rule), and some children may exceed expectations…so don't hold your child back if he or she really wants to read a particular book (even if it may appear to be too challenging).

Remember, if students do some of these simple activities, they can prevent the typical four to six weeks of learning loss due to the "summer slide." And since spelling, vocabulary and reading skills are vulnerable areas, be sure to encourage your child to maintain his or her current literacy level…it will go a long way come September!

SUMMER IS HERE! KEEP YOUR CHILD'S WRITING SKILLS SHARP WITH ONLINE GAMES

Like Reading and math, free online activities exist for all subjects... and writing is no exception. Check out the following free interactive writing activities, puzzles, quizzes and games that reinforce writing skills and encourage creativity:

Primary Level (K-2nd Grade)

Story Writing Game

In this game, the child fills in the blanks of a short story. The challenge is for the storyteller to choose words that fit the kind of story that has been selected. For example, if the child chooses to tell a ghost story, then he or she must select words for each blank that would be appropriate for a scary tale. http://www.funenglishgames.com/writinggames/story.html

Opinions Quiz for Critical Thinking

Practice developing logical reasons to support a thesis with this interactive activity. Students read the stated opinion, such as, "We should have longer recess because..." The child must then select all of the possible reasons from a list that would support the given statement. The challenge lies with the fact that each statement may have more than one possible answer, and to receive credit, the student must select all correct responses. This game is best suited for older primary students. http://www.netrover.com/~kingskid/Opinion/opinion.html

Interactives: Sequence

Allow your child to practice ordering events with this interactive version of the fairy tale, Cinderella. The child looks at several pictures from the story and must drag them to the bottom of the screen to put the events in chronological order. When the player mouses over each scene from the story, a sentence describing the image appears and is read aloud to the student. Once the events are in order, the student can learn more about the plot and other story elements with the accompanying tutorials and lessons. http://www.learner.org/interactives/story/sequence.html

WEBINAR "CLIFF NOTES" FOR BEATING SUMMER ACADEMIC LOSS: AN INFORMATIVE GUIDE TO PARENTS

The "Summer Slide"

First, it's important to understand the implications of "summer slide" – otherwise known as summer learning loss. Research has shown that some students who take standardized tests in the fall could have lost up to 4-6 weeks of learning each school year (when compared with test results from the previous spring). This means that teachers end up dedicating the first month of each new school year for reviewing material before they can move onto any new content and concepts.

The three areas that suffer most from summer learning loss are in the areas of vocabulary/reading, spelling, and math. In Stop! In the Name of Education: Prevent Summer Learning Loss With 7 Simple Steps, we discussed some activities parents could use with children to prevent summer slide. Let's add to that list with even more ways to keep children engaged and learning – all summer long.

Be sure to check out:

•Your Child's School

Talk to child's teacher, and tell him or her that you'd like to work on your child's academics over the summer. Most teachers will have many suggestions for you.

In addition to the classroom teacher as a resource, talk to the front office staff and guidance counselors. Reading lists and summer programs that are organized through the school district may be available for your family, and these staff members can usually point you in the right direction.

•Your Community

A quick Google search for "free activities for kids in (insert your town's name)" will yield results of possible educational experiences and opportunities in your area. Some towns offer "dollar days", park lunches, and local arts and entertainment.

You may even wish to involve your child in the research process to find fun, affordable memberships and discounts to use at area attractions. For New Jerseyans and Coloradans, check out www.funnewjersey.com and www.colorado.com for ideas.

Of course, don't forget your local library! In addition to books, you can borrow movies and audiobooks, check out the latest issue of your favorite magazine, and get free Internet access on the library's computers. Most libraries offer a plethora of other educational choices, too – from book clubs and author visits to movie nights and crafts classes, you're sure to find something at your local branch that your child will enjoy.

•Stores

This is an extremely engaging activity – and your child won't even know he or she is learning! For grocery shopping, ask your child to write the list while you dictate. At the store, your son/daughter can locate the items and keep a cost tally to stay within a specified budget. At the checkout, you can have a contest to see whose estimate of the final bill is most accurate – and then reward the winner!

You may wish to plan a home improvement project or plant a garden: for this, your child can make the list, research the necessary materials, and then plan and execute the project after a visit to your local home improvement store. All of these activities involve those three critical areas of spelling, vocabulary/reading, and math.

•The Kitchen

This is one of the best places to try new things – by researching new foods, recipes, and discussing healthy food choices – while practicing math skills (such as measuring ingredients, doubling recipes, etc.). Your child may also enjoy reading about new cultures and ethnicities and then trying out some new menu items from those cultures.

•The Television

TV doesn't have to be mind numbing … when used appropriately. You can watch sports with your child to review stats and make predictions; watch documentaries; or tune into the History Channel, Discovery, National Geographic, HGTV, and more. Anything that teaches, helps your child discover new interests, and promotes learning new things together is fair game.

As an extension, you may decide to research whether or not the show portrays accurate information. And for those children who really get "into" a certain topic, you can enrich their learning by taking related trips to the museum, doing Internet research, and checking out books from the library that tie into the topic of interest.

•Movies

Movies can be educational, too, if you debrief with your child afterwards. Schedule a family movie night, and then discuss how realistic the movie was, what the messages were, etc.

For book-based movies (such as Judy Moody, Harry Potter, Percy Jackson, etc.), you could read the book together first, and then view the movie version. Comparing and contrasting the two is another terrific educational way to enjoy time together and work on your child's reasoning skills.

Note: www.imdb.com and www.commonsensemedia.org are great sites for movie recommendations and movie reviews for kids and families.

•Games

Playing games promotes taking turns, reading and math skills, and strategy development. Scour yard sales for affordable board games like Scrabble, Monopoly, Uno, Battleship, and Qwirkle.

Don't forget about non-board games, like those found on the Wii, Nintendo, Xbox, and other gaming consoles. You'll still want to choose wisely and limit your child's screen time, but these electronic versions of popular (and new) games mirror the way kids think ... while focusing on reading and math skills. For more ideas, Google "education apps" for suggestions.

•Books, books, books!

Of course, nothing beats reading for maintaining skills. When you can connect your child with a book that is of interest to him or her, it can be fun for your child, build confidence, and improve fluency.

To help your child find a book that's "just right", use the five-finger rule: choose a page from a possible book and have your child read that page. Every time he or she encounters an unknown word, put up a finger. If your child exceeds five fingers (that is, five unknown words), that book is probably too challenging and he or she may wish to pass on it.

For reluctant readers, consider non-book reading options, like:magazines (such as Ranger Rick, American Girl, Discovery Kids, and Sports Illustrated for Kids), cereal boxes, billboards, current events, closed captioning, and karaoke. If you keep your eyes open, you'll find there are many natural reading opportunities that surround us every day.

Whatever you do, remember to keep it fun. Summer is a time for rest and rejuvenation, and learning doesn't always have to be scheduled. In fact, some of the most educational experiences are unplanned.

Visit lumoslearning.com/parents/summer-program for more information.

Valuable Learning Experiences: A Summer Activity Guide for Parents

Soon school will be out of session, leaving the summer free for adventure and relaxation. However, it's important to also use the summer for learning activities. Giving your son or daughter opportunities to keep learning can result in more maturity, self-growth, curiosity, and intelligence. Read on to learn some ways to make the most of this summer.

Read
Summer is the perfect time to get some extra reading accomplished. Youth can explore books about history, art, animals, and other interests, or they can read classic novels that have influenced people for decades. A lot of libraries have summer fun reading programs which give children, teens, and adults little weekly prizes for reading books. You can also offer a reward, like a $25 gift card, if your child reads a certain amount of books.

Travel
"The World is a book and those who do not travel read only a page." This quote by Saint Augustine illustrates why travel is so important for a student (and even you!). Travel opens our eyes to new cultures, experiences, and challenges. When you travel, you see commonalities and differences between cultures.

Professor Adam Galinsky of Columbia Business School, who has researched travel benefits, said in a Quartz article that travel can help a child develop compassion and empathy: "Engaging with another culture helps kids recognize that their own egocentric way of looking at the world is not the only way of being in the world."

If the student in your life constantly complains about not having the newest iPhone, how would they feel seeing a child in a third-world country with few possessions? If you child is disrespectful and self-centered, what would they learn going to Japan and seeing a culture that promotes respect and otherness instead of self-centeredness?

If you can't afford to travel to another country, start a family travel fund everyone can contribute to and in the meantime, travel somewhere new locally! Many people stay in the area they live instead of exploring. Research attractions in your state and nearby states to plan a short road trip to fun and educational places!

Visit Museums
You can always take your children to visit museums. Spending some quality time at a museum can enhance curiosity because children can learn new things, explore their interests, or see exhibits expanding upon school subjects they recently studied. Many museums have seasonal exhibits, so research special exhibits nearby. For example, "Titanic: The Artifact Exhibition" has been making its way to various museums in the United States. It contains items recovered from the Titanic as well as interactive activities and displays explaining the doomed ship's history and tragic demise. This year, the exhibit is visiting Las Vegas, Orlando, and Waco.

Work

A final learning suggestion for the summer is for students to get a job, internship, or volunteer position. Such jobs can help with exploring career options. For example, if your child is thinking of becoming a vet, they could walk dogs for neighbors, or if your child wants to start their own business, summer is the perfect time to make and sell products.

Not only will a job or volunteer work look good on college applications, but it will also teach your children valuable life lessons that can result in more maturity and responsibility. You could enhance the experience by teaching them accounting and illustrating real world problems to them, like budgeting money for savings and bills.

The above suggestions are just four of the many ways you can help learning continue for your child or children all summer long. Experience and seeing things first-hand are some of the most important ways that students can learn, so we hope you find the above suggestions helpful in designing a fun, educational, and rewarding summer that will have benefits in and out of the classroom.

Additional Information

What if I buy more than one Lumos Study Program?

Step 1

Visit the URL and login to your account.
http://www.lumoslearning.com

Step 2

Click on 'My tedBooks' under the "Account" tab.
Place the Book Access Code and submit.

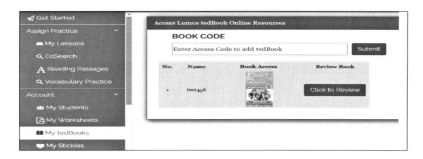

Step 3

To add the new book for a registered student, choose the
◎ Existing Student button and select the student and submit.

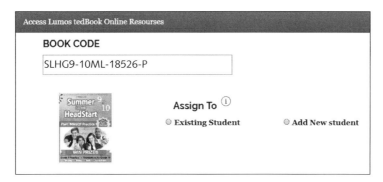

To add the new book for a new student, choose the ◎ Add New student
button and complete the student registration.

Lumos tedBooks for State Assessments Practice

Lumos tedBook for standardized test practice provides necessary grade-specific state assessment practice and skills mastery. Each tedBook includes hundreds of standards-aligned practice questions and online summative assessments that mirror actual state tests.

The workbook provides students access to thousands of valuable learning resources such as worksheets, videos, apps, books, and much more.

Lumos Learning tedBooks for State Assessment	
SBAC Math & ELA Practice Book	CA, CT, DE, HI, ID, ME, MI, MN, NV, ND, OR, WA, WI
NJSLA Math & ELA Practice Book	NJ
ACT Aspire Math & ELA Practice Book	AL, AR
IAR Math & ELA Practice Book	IL
FSA Math & ELA Practice Book	FL
PARCC Math & ELA Practice Book	DC, NM
GMAS Math & ELA Practice Book	GA
NYST Math & ELA Practice Book	NY
ILEARN Math & ELA Practice Book	IN
LEAP Math & ELA Practice Book	LA
MAP Math & ELA Practice Book	MO
MAAP Math & ELA Practice Book	MS
AZM2 Math & ELA Practice Book	AZ
MCAP Math & ELA Practice Book	MD
OST Math & ELA Practice Book	OH
MCAS Math & ELA Practice Book	MA
CMAS Math & ELA Practice Book	CO
TN Ready Math & ELA Practice Book	TN
STAAR Math & ELA Practice Book	TX
NMMSSA Math & ELA Practice Book	NM

Available

- At Leading book stores
- www.lumoslearning.com/a/lumostedbooks